151 W9-DEE-821

The Mystery Library

Urban Legends

Stuart A. Kallen

LUCENT BOOKS

An imprint of Thomson Gale, a part of The Thomson Corporation

THOMSON

™

GALE

Detroit • New York • San Francisco • San Diego • New Haven, Conn. • Waterville, Maine • London • Munich

LIBRARY OF CONGRESS CATALOGING-IN-PUBLICATION DATA

Kallen, Stuart A., 1955–
    Urban legends / by Stuart A. Kallen.
        p. cm. — (Mystery library)
    Includes bibliographical references and index.
    ISBN 1-59018-830-6 (alk. paper)
    Contents: Animal myths—Food fears and fantasies—Government conspiracies—Legends of stage and screen—Criminal acts and gruesome legends.
    1. Urban folklore—United States. 2. Legends—United States. I. Title. II. Series.
    GR105.5.K35 2005
    398.2'0973'091732—dc22
                                                                          2005013868

Printed in the United States of America

Contents

Foreword

In Shakespeare's immortal play, *Hamlet*, the young Danish aristocrat Horatio has clearly been astonished and disconcerted by his encounter with a ghostlike apparition on the castle battlements. "There are more things in heaven and earth," his friend Hamlet assures him, "than are dreamt of in your philosophy."

Many people today would readily agree with Hamlet that the world and the vast universe surrounding it are teeming with wonders and oddities that remain largely outside the realm of present human knowledge or understanding. How did the universe begin? What caused the dinosaurs to become extinct? Was the lost continent of Atlantis a real place or merely legendary? Does a monstrous creature lurk beneath the surface of Scotland's Loch Ness? These are only a few of the intriguing questions that remain unanswered, despite the many great strides made by science in recent centuries.

Lucent Books' Mystery Library series is dedicated to exploring these and other perplexing, sometimes bizarre, and often disturbing or frightening wonders. Each volume in the series presents the best-known tales, incidents, and evidence surrounding the topic in question. Also included are the opinions and theories of scientists and other experts who have attempted to unravel and solve the ongoing mystery. And supplementing this information is a lengthy list of sources for further reading, providing the reader with the means to pursue the topic further.

The Mystery Library will satisfy every young reader's fascination for the unexplained. As one of history's greatest scientists, physicist Albert Einstein, put it:

The most beautiful thing we can experience is the mysterious. It is the source of all true art and science. He to whom this emotion is a stranger, who can no longer wonder and stand rapt in awe, is as good as dead: his eyes are closed.

Stories, Rumors, and Urban Legends

Many people have heard the stories about alligators living in the sewers of New York City or the woman who found a deep-fried rat among her pieces of Kentucky Fried Chicken. Such stories are known as urban legends, contemporary legends, or modern myths. They often have a basis in reality and have been generated in multiple versions that have been repeated countless times. According to Barbara Mikkelson and David P. Mikkelson on the Urban Legends Reference Pages Web site, the term *urban legend* is a catchall name for "common fallacies, misinformation, old wives' tales, strange news stories, rumors [and] celebrity gossip."[1]

Urban legends can cover a wide range of topics, most of them with bizarre twists concerning common matters that involve traveling, shopping, eating, babysitting, criminal acts, accidents, business practices, and the government. They often conclude with a horrific, vengeful, or nauseating finale.

Folklorists, people who study traditional stories from long ago, point out that urban legends are similar in some ways to stories passed along by ancient Greeks, and most likely, the first humans who ever lived on earth. For example, in ancient Greek tales, a three-headed dog named Cerberus stood watch over the entrance to Hades. In a Celtic myth from Ireland, a boy kills a hound and so must take his place as a guard dog. In English folklore, there are dozens of stories about phantom black dogs, ghosts in the night that foretell of death.

In ancient times, legends were spread by word of mouth. By the Middle Ages, they were recorded in handwritten

An ancient Greek pot depicts Heracles doing battle with Cerberus, the mythical three-headed dog that guarded the entrance to the underworld.

In 2001 a report of Britney Spears's death appeared on a Web page falsely identifying itself as the BBC News.

books and letters. In the last century, urban legends were circulated in chain letters, printed on flyers, and detailed in newspaper and magazine articles. Today, computers have accelerated the spread of such tales to unprecedented levels. In the twenty-first century, urban legends travel around the world in a matter of minutes to millions of computer users and e-mail subscribers.

Psychological Fears

Although they are now spread by high-tech tools, urban legends often focus on common concerns and deep psychological fears. For example, there are few people in modern times who would not cringe in horror at the thought of eating a fried rat or discovering a homicidal maniac under the bed. These hidden personal fears are amplified by real-world events covered endlessly in newspapers, magazines, and on television. It is little wonder, then, that people have nightmares about senseless slaughter, tainted food, kidnapping, torture, and other frightening subjects that are ever-present in the media. Perhaps it is simply a psychological survival tactic that impels people to incorporate these horrors into urban legends. By turning a deep terror into a fictional story or even a joke, the dread can be packaged into a neat narrative in the mind. This takes away the power of an impending fear and allows a person to mentally cope. These psychological dynamics are explained by Linda Dégh in *Legend and Belief:*

> [Urban legends] deal with the most crucial questions of the world and human life. They attack these questions: Is the order of the world really as we learned to know it? Can we expect that life will run its course as we were taught it should? Do we know all the forces that will regulate the universe and our life, or are there hidden dimensions that can divert the casual rational flow of things? And if there are unknown forces, can they be identified, changed, avoided or exploited to our benefit?[2]

Girl Hatches Cockroaches in Her Mouth

Those who pass along urban legends swear that the stories are true, that they happened to a friend, or a "friend of a friend"[3] or as folklorists like to say a FOAF. In this way, urban legends differ from fairy tales and parables, which most often happened long ago to kings and princesses, mythical gods, or legendary monsters. Instead, urban legends are said to be real events that happened to real people in recent times. And the underlying message is that the horrible event might someday actually happen to people hearing the story.

To many, the origins of urban legends are a mystery. It is hard to imagine an anonymous person sitting at a computer composing an e-mail, as in one case, about a girl who hatched cockroaches in her mouth after eating a taco from a popular fast-food restaurant. Yet that e-mail has been circulating on the Internet since the late 1990s, and continues to do so today.

This cockroach story is mysterious in other ways. For example, it is unknown how it "morphed" from a true story into an urban myth. The *New York Times* actually ran a story on November 19, 1998, with the headline "City Said to Use More Pesticides than Farm Counties." The story made no mention of fast-food restaurants or roaches found in food. It simply stated that people in New York City used more pesticides to kill roaches and rats than farmers did in rural New York. There were only two references to roaches and

Although cockroaches are sometimes found in fast food, the story of roach eggs hatching in one's mouth after eating infested fast food is an urban legend.

none about an unfortunate girl who allegedly woke up with a mouthful of the insects. Yet, according to those who have researched the story, someone illogically decided to take that story and turn it into an urban legend that played on common fears.

The cockroach story is surprisingly believable for reasons explained by the acknowledged expert in urban legends, Jan Harold Brunvand, writing in *The Vanishing Hitchhiker:* "[The] wide distribution and acceptance of [this] and other similar [urban legends] teach us something about how [people] react to situations involving corporate or individual negligence of health and cleanliness standards."[4]

Like most urban legends, the story contains a grain of truth—cockroaches can be a problem in the city, especially in restaurants. Despite the scientific fact that they cannot hatch in a person's mouth, the legend unaccountably took on a life of its own. There are few explanations as to why this happens, but the phenomenon is widespread among all types of people. As contemporary-legend folklorist Stewart F. Sanderson told the Folklore Society in London, urban legends are repeated by "old and young, well read and barely literate, educationally privileged and educationally deprived."[5]

With a popularity that reaches nearly every segment of society—and indeed across the globe—urban legends have long been a part of human interaction. People may simply use an urban legend as an icebreaker, like talking about the weather, as a way to interact with another person. Whatever the case, tellers of urban legends often take delight in amusing or nauseating their friends. From ancient Greece to modern America, people seem to love good stories in which evildoers run amok, the arrogant are ridiculed, or tragedy befalls an innocent person. Perhaps the biggest mystery is why people have a such a deep need to conjure up these stories. As long as people think and imagine, urban legends will likely remain an important part of human conversation.

Chapter 1

Animal Myths

Many people love animals and, judging by the sheer numbers of urban legends concerning animals, people also seem to love strange stories about dogs, rabbits, spiders, alligators, and dozens of other creatures. The love most people have for animals rarely extends to those in urban legends, however; it is a rare story in which the critter is not at the center of a horrible event. As Barbara Mikkelson and David P. Mikkelson write: "If [an animal] isn't the object of some unfortunate mishap, he's being treated cruelly, causing a calamity, being unceremoniously disposed of, or forming the main course of someone's meal. And when the animal's turn to be the star of the story comes, it's usually because he's attacked some unsuspecting human being."[6]

People seem eager to believe animal legends for several reasons. To some, they are simply good stories, remarkable or amusing, which makes them fun to repeat. Others see messages behind animal legends that confirm their world view, for example, that some people can be exceptionally cruel or stupid around their pets. Then there are those who may doubt the veracity of a legend but pass it along as a warning to others just in case the story is true.

Fables and Fairy Tales

Whatever the reason for their popularity, animals have long been at the center of myths and fables. Some have been told for thousands of years. These stories often symbolize the ways that human beings cope with the world, or they may explain why things are the way they are. Such myths can form the basis for a society's philosophy and religion. In tales from ancient Greece, animals are often remarkable in ways that allow them to convey prevalent philosophies and beliefs. The animals are mythical creatures such as dragons, magical animals such as a bird that always tells the truth, or animals that possess human traits like bravery or deceitfulness. Psychologist Marie-Louise von Franz spent much of her life studying the world's animal folklore and discovered a common theme running through the stories no matter

In this medieval illustration, a dragon devours a saint. Legends and myths often include animals, both real and mythical.

13

where they are from. Whenever an animal in a fable offers advice, those who fail to heed it are doomed, as she writes:

> [One] must never hurt the helpful animal in fairy tales. . . . [You] may temporarily disobey the advice of the helpful fox or wolf or cat. But if basically you go against it, if you do not listen to the helpful animal or bird, or whatever it is, if any animal gives you advice and you don't follow it, then you are finished. [7]

An old Native American tale in which a mouse fails to reward a helpful fox illustrates von Franz's point. In this story, an angry mouse confronts a buffalo that is stomping down the grass where the tiny creature hides from preda-

The Ancient Practice of Transmitting Lore

Jan Harold Brunvand is a renowned expert in urban legends; he has written more than six books on the subject. In *The Vanishing Hitchhiker*, Brunvand analyzes the age-old human fascination with legends:

When we follow the ancient practice of informally transmitting "lore"—wisdom, knowledge, or accepted modes of behavior—by word of mouth and customary example from person to person, we do not concentrate on the form or content of our folklore; instead, we simply listen to information that others tell us and then pass it on—more or less accurately—to other listeners. In this stream of unselfconscious oral tradition the information that acquires a clear story line is called narrative folklore, and those stories alleged to be true are legends. This, in broad summary, is the typical process of legend formation and transmission as it has existed from time immemorial and continues to

operate today. It works about the same way whether the legendary plot concerns a dragon in a cave or a mouse in a Coke bottle.

It might seem unlikely that legends—urban legends at that—would continue to be created in an age of widespread literacy, rapid mass communications, and restless travel. . . . A moment's reflection, however, reminds us of the many weird, fascinating, but unverified rumors and tales that so frequently come to our ears—killers and madmen on the loose, shocking or funny personal experiences, unsafe manufactured products, and many other unexplained mysteries of daily life. . . . The lack of verification in no way diminishes the appeal urban legends have for us. We enjoy them merely as stories, and we tend at least to half-believe them as possibly accurate reports. And the legends . . . reflect many of the hopes, fears, and anxieties of our time.

tors. The mouse challenges the buffalo to a fight, and when the great animal laughs and refuses to leave, the mouse jumps in the buffalo's ear and gnaws at its brains until it is driven mad with pain. After running in circles to dislodge the mouse, the great beast falls down dead.

Having accomplished this incredible task, the mouse comes to believe that it is now the king of all prairie creatures. A red fox appears, however, and tells the mouse he is having a bad day hunting. The fox asks the mouse if he will share the meat, but the tiny creature demands that the fox butcher the buffalo and cut the pieces up into small, mouse-sized bites. The fox is hungry, but obliging and helpful. He indicates that sharing is a good character trait and does what the mouse orders. When the task is done, the mouse gives the fox a single, very small serving. The hungry fox asks for more, but the mouse arrogantly refuses. Exasperated, the fox jumps on the tiny rodent and eats it. The moral of the story, according to the Native American Lore Index Web site, is: "If you are proud and selfish you will lose all in the end."[8]

The tale of the buffalo and the field mouse is a parable, that is, a story with a moral lesson, most likely told to children to warn them against pride and egoism. While the story is probably more than five hundred years old, folklorists consider many modern urban legends to be parables with similar, if less obvious, messages.

One Dog's Tale

The urban legend called the Choking Doberman is an example of a tale with a lesson. It concerns a woman who came home one afternoon to find her Doberman pinscher lying on the floor gagging and choking. She rushed the dog to the veterinarian, but the pet doctor was unable to determine exactly what was blocking the dog's windpipe. As the dog grew weaker, the vet told the woman he would have to operate immediately. He advised her to go home and await his phone call. Jan Harold Brunvand picks up the story in *The Mexican Pet:*

> The woman drove directly back home, and as soon as she got out of her car, she heard her telephone ringing ["ringing off the hook!" people say when they tell this story]. She opened her front door and grabbed the phone; it was the vet, highly excited. "Listen carefully," he said in a tone of great urgency. "I want you to hang up the phone when I tell you to; then don't say a word, but turn around and run straight out the door again. Go to a neighbor's and wait for the police to arrive! I've called them. Now! Don't say a word and don't hesitate, just get right out of there!" [9]

The frightened woman did as she was told. A few minutes later, police arrived and explained the urgency. The vet had found two human fingers stuck in the dog's throat. He assumed someone had broken into the woman's house and the dog had bitten the robber's fingers off. The police then searched the house and found a robber in shock and cowering in an upstairs bedroom closet, trying to stop the blood gushing from his right hand, where two fingers had been bitten off.

The obvious moral lesson behind the Choking Doberman story is that breaking into houses is not only bad but also could have very serious consequences to a person's health. The story mimics parables in another manner: Many parables contain heroic, wounded animals that suffer for a human being. And while the similarities to ancient legends may end there, the Choking Doberman shares subject matter with several other modern stories of urban folklore. In many, an urgent message or warning is excitedly delivered by telephone. Countless urban legends also contain robbers, rapists, or murderers hidden upstairs in a closet, in the backseat of a car, or somewhere else both familiar and frightening.

In a common urban legend, a Doberman chokes after biting off fingers from the hand of an intruder entering the home.

"Police Can't Put a Finger on the Story"

Like many urban legends, the Choking Doberman has an obvious basis in reality. Dogs are known to attack robbers and others who would harm their owners. In this case, the Doberman story was actually reported as a news item from Las Vegas on June 24, 1981, by a weekly newspaper, *New Times*, in Phoenix, Arizona. The paper did, however, add the disclaimer that the story was told to them by a nameless employee of a large industrial plant in Phoenix. A *New Times* reporter made a call to the Las Vegas *Sun* but was unable to confirm the authenticity of the story. Upon further research, the reporter discovered that Las Vegas police had no record of a three-fingered thief or a choking Doberman.

Despite the fact that the story seemed to be false, it mysteriously made its way across the country to dozens of cities. In Georgia, reporter Ron Hudspeth of the *Atlanta Journal* wrote that at least six people, all of them somber and earnest, called to tell him the story. However, none of the callers could give details such as the woman's name or where she lived. In Nebraska, on July 4, 1981, the *Lincoln Journal* made light of the incident, writing: "Police can't put [a] finger on the story."[10]

In the following months, the urban legend of the Choking Doberman was reported in the *Tampa Bay Star;* the Benton Harbor, Michigan, *Herald-Palladium;* the Hamilton, Ontario, *Spectator;* the *Los Angeles Herald Examiner;* and by the Associated Press in New York and Seattle. Most made jokes of the story, saying it was "hard to swallow" or that "[a] reporter's dogged search reveals some hard-bitten truths."[11]

Many newspaper reporters were not fooled by the Choking Doberman story. However, the veracity of the story was unquestioned by thousands of people who repeated it at school, work, and social gatherings. Brunvand, speaking at a folklore conference in Sheffield, England, commented on this mysterious aspect of the urban legends:

> [Published] reports . . . have clearly stated that The Choking Doberman story is untrue—calling it rumor, legend, myth and the like. Yet most folk narrators of the story tell it as true, although they may mention in validation that they read it in a paper, heard it on the radio or have it firsthand from a friend who had it from a reliable source. Also, most narrators assert that the incident occurred either in their own city or town, or else in a nearby one.[12]

Brunvand's point was confirmed by Los Angeles columnist Digby Diehl, who heard the Choking Doberman story repeated at a cocktail party. This version was about a German shepherd that chewed three fingers off a large, menacing burglar in the nearby upscale Brentwood neighborhood. Everyone at the dinner party was amazed by the story and shocked by a crime that hit so close to home. Diehl wrote that he retold the story several times himself in the following week. At later dinner parties, however, the columnist heard the story again and again, only it was reported as having happened in San Francisco, Long Island, New York, and several other Southern Californian cities such as Palos Verdes and Montecito. Finally realizing that the story was false, Diehl wrote, "part of the power of this folklore is that at the time of the telling we believe the story to be true."[13]

An Incompetent Mutt

While the story of the finger-eating Doberman is a tale with a helpful creature, many urban legends have malicious or dangerous animals. Some are harmful by accident, such as the seeing eye dog named Lucky. According to an item that was widely viewed on the Internet in the late 1990s,

The Brave Dog Gellert

The concept of a pet who suffers after sacrificing for his owner is a common theme in urban legends, even those from ancient times. In *Curious Myths of the Middle Ages*, written in 1866, Sabine Baring-Gould relates one old legend that was told in different versions in eighteenth-century Russia and France, sixth-century India, and even ancient Greece. The following is from the sixteenth century and is still told in the town of Beddgelert, Wales:

The Welsh Prince Llewellyn had a noble deerhound, Gellert, whom he trusted to watch the cradle of his baby son whilst he himself was absent. One day, on his return, to his intense horror, he beheld the cradle empty and upset, the clothes dabbled with blood, and Gellert's mouth dripping with gore. Concluding hastily that the hound had proved unfaithful, had fallen on the child and devoured it,—in a paroxysm of rage the prince drew his sword and slew the dog. Next instant the cry of the babe from behind the cradle showed him that the child was uninjured, and, on looking further, Llewellyn discovered the body of a huge wolf, which had entered the house to seize and devour the child, but which had been kept off and killed by the brave dog Gellert.

In his self-reproach and grief, the prince erected a stately monument to Gellert, and called the place where he was buried after the poor hound's name.

Lucky was such a bad seeing eye dog that he killed four of his owners. The story was reprinted in the Web site Urban Legends Reference Pages:

> "We will not have him put down. Lucky is basically a damn good guide dog," Ernst Gerber, a dog trainer from Wuppertal [Germany] told reporters. "He just needs a little brush-up on some elementary skills, that's all."

> Gerber admitted to the press conference that Lucky, a German shepherd guide-dog for the blind, had so far been responsible for the deaths of all four of his previous owners. "I admit it's not an impressive record on paper. He led his first owner in front of a bus, and the second off the end of a pier. He actually pushed his third owner off a railway platform just as the Cologne to Frankfurt express was approaching and he walked his fourth owner into heavy traffic, before abandoning him and running away to safety. But, apart from epileptic fits, he has a lovely temperament. And guide dogs are difficult to train these days."

> Asked if Lucky's fifth owner would be told about his previous record, Gerber replied: "No. It would make them nervous, and would make Lucky nervous. And when Lucky gets nervous he's liable to do something silly."[14]

Lucky's story was reported in 1993 in a magazine called *Europa Times* and was mentioned in other major media sources. The story is typical of many urban legends in which malicious animals harm—or kill—a person, especially someone innocent, helpful, or with a disability. Such stories often focus on a clueless human being who aids the animal or creates a situation in which the animal can cause harm. In this case, the legend features Ernst Gerber, a dog trainer who ap-

A guide dog lies at its master's feet during a dinner party. Guide dogs for the blind frequently feature in urban legends about service animals that turn on their helpless owners.

parently has no problem placing the dangerous seeing eye dog with a string of hapless people. Since this legend omits the names of the people killed, the name of the organization that Gerber works for, and the date and time of the alleged press conference, it is an easy story for scholars of urban legends to debunk. In addition, anyone investigating the truth of the story would learn that seeing eye dogs are rigorously trained for eighteen months, and then trained further with their future owners. Of course those who spread such urban legends care little for facts when they interfere with a good story.

Unbearable Bears

Another story with a human being of dubious intelligence, a dangerous animal, and an innocent victim comes from an unnamed national park. The story, said to have been presented on National Public Radio (NPR), concerns a report about people who visit the park. A park ranger allegedly told a reporter that people often want to get their pictures taken standing next to bears. The ranger said that to do so, one man smeared honey all over his young child's head to attract the bear for a photograph. When the bear smelled the honey, the child's face was viciously mauled. The ranger purportedly was in tears when telling of the incident on the radio.

While people visiting national parks often do unwise things when snapping pictures, such as taunting bears, bison, and moose, no one has ever been unintelligent enough to use a honey-smeared child as bear bait. But a good urban legend is hard to stop, and this story has been making the rounds for at least fifty years. There is a grain of truth to the

The story of this bear cub rescued from a New Mexico forest fire in 1950 may have been the source of the urban legend of a child-mauling bear.

story, however. In New Mexico in 1950, a two-month-old bear cub was rescued from a forest fire. The small creature was taken to Santa Fe, where a photographer wanted to take a picture of the cub with the young daughter of the game warden who rescued it. To get the heartwarming shot, which was published in several national magazines, the photographer smeared honey on the little girl's chin and took a picture of the cub licking it off.

How the story morphed into a mauled child remains a mystery. However, like many legends, there is a moral to the story. Every year dozens of people (and their children) really do get mangled by bears in America's national parks. While the mauling of a honey-smeared child has never been reported, the story shows that it is wise to stay away from wild bears.

Exploding Pickups and Other Revenge Tales

Animal accidents frequently appear in the annals of urban legends, and revenge is central to a number of these tales. In many urban legends, vengeful animals wreak havoc on dimwitted people. As with the traditional fairy tales studied by von Franz, these stories make the point that cruelty to animals might exact a high price from those who perpetrate such acts.

The tale known as Rabbit's Revenge was reported in the Australian magazine *New Scientist* in August 1984. The story begins with two hunters, hundreds of miles from the nearest town, who manage to catch a live rabbit. Drunk and bored, the two hunters decide to strap a stick of dynamite to the rabbit's back, light the fuse, and let it run free until it explodes. The plan goes awry when the frightened rabbit runs for cover under their expensive new pickup truck, which is demolished when the dynamite detonates.

A slightly different, more detailed version of the tale comes from a 2002 Internet story. In this case, the two hunters are

The Poodle in the Microwave

Animals are often treated cruelly in urban legends, usually by dim-witted owners who are clueless as to the pain they are about to cause their innocent pet. The Poodle in the Microwave is an urban legend classic, explained by Brandon Toropov in *The Complete Idiot's Guide to Urban Legends:*

[The microwaved poodle story is a] grim but apt message for human beings (that they are capable of heedlessly destroying someone or something they love). [This] may account for its popularity.

In the story, a woman gives her beloved poodle a shampoo but finds herself frustrated when she can't dry him off quickly enough with a standard towel. Then, after catching a glimpse of the microwave oven in her kitchen, she has a brainstorm. She'll pop the pooch in the oven, punch High, zap the animal for a minute or so, and be ready to roll.

When she does so, however, disaster unfolds. The poodle, alas, explodes, thereby providing an important, if grisly, object lesson in the improper use of modern cooking tools—and supplying the requisite "yuck factor" necessary for an enduring urban legend.

in Michigan, have a brand new $42,500 Lincoln Navigator with monthly payments of $550. The two men take their dog, a black Labrador, and go duck hunting in the dead of winter. They drive their SUV out to the middle of a frozen lake. As most hunters know, ducks are attracted to open water in the winter, so the men decide to use a stick of dynamite to blow a hole in the ice. One hunter lights the dynamite, and the other throws it as far as he can. The dog, a retriever, thinks the men are playing fetch. He picks up the dynamite and runs toward them. Hoping to stop the dog, the frightened men fire their shotgun at the confused animal. They miss, but the terrified dog runs under the SUV, which explodes; a hole is blown in the ice through which the fiery wreck falls to the bottom of the lake. The insurance company later refused to pay for the Navigator, and the owner was forced to make payments of $550 on his demolished SUV for the next six years.

This urban legend, like many others, contains details that might give a clue to its truthfulness. Since the name of the lake and the names of the hunters are unknown, the story might be false. On the other hand, the story works because the stunt sounds like something that two dim-witted, drunk hunters might actually try. Whether or not someone, somewhere actually had their truck blown up by a frightened animal carrying a stick of dynamite remains a mystery. The urban legend, however, has been reported as having happened in a half dozen American states and several different countries.

Albino Alligators

While some urban legends feature domestic animals wreaking havoc in wild places, others concern wild animals causing problems in urban areas. Those stories, with spiders, snakes, alligators, and other crawling creatures, play on common fears. They also reflect city dwellers' widespread fear of wild creatures stinging, biting, or even eating them. As Swedish folklorist Bengt Klintberg explains, as a consequence of this terror, such tales "have come to assume mythical proportions in our narrative traditions."[15]

The fear many people have of large reptiles, alligators in particular, is central to an urban legend that has circulated for at least seventy years. This persistent legend holds that tourists from New York City who visited Florida brought baby alligators home for their children to raise as pets. Unfortunately, the baby gators were destined to quickly grow into dangerous predators, at which point their owners resorted to flushing them down the toilet to get rid of them. It seems that a few of these hastily disposed-of creatures actually survived in the damp darkness of the New York sewer system and began to breed, feasting on the abundant rats and an occasional unfortunate sewer worker. Today, it is said, there are scattered colonies of full-grown alligators living under the streets of New York City. Some say the animals are blind and albino, or white skinned, having lost their eyesight and the pigment in their hides due to the constant darkness in which they dwell.

The source of this story is a mystery, but it has been repeated countless times. Some trace the source of this urban legend to a nineteenth-century English tale that alleged that black pigs were living in the sewers of Hampstead. Others believe the story started on February 10, 1935, when the *New York Times* reported that an alligator was pulled from a sewer on East 123rd Street. This story did not mention, however, that people flushed alligators down the toilet. In fact, the paper reported that the alligator probably fell off a ship recently returned from the Florida Everglades. At the time, no one assumed it was a denizen of the sewer system.

The Alligators in the Sewer story might have fallen by the wayside were it not for a 1959 book called *The World Beneath the City* by Robert Daley. This work, a history of public utilities in New York City, quoted a retired sewer district foreman named Teddy May, who claimed that during the 1930s he investigated workers' reports of subterranean gators and saw a colony of them with his own eyes. He also claimed to have personally seen to their eradication. Records do confirm that May worked for the city during that time, but whether he was telling the truth is unknown.

Whatever the case, the legend has been mentioned in countless cartoons, children's books, comic books, and even a film called *Alligator*. Not willing to let a commercial opportunity pass, the New York City Department of Environmental Protection's Bureau of Wastewater Treatment sells T-shirts with a drawing of an alligator wearing sunglasses and crawling out of a manhole. The caption on the T-shirts reads, "The Legend Lives."[16]

As is the case with many urban legends there is an associated story. During the 1960s, people commonly flushed marijuana down the toilet when police raided their homes and apartments. As a result, a particularly potent strain of

albino marijuana called New York White was rumored to be growing in the sewers. The problem for marijuana users was that those who tried to harvest the marijuana might be eaten by the alligators that lurked below.

While the source of these stories remains enigmatic, it is known that marijuana plants, like alligators, need sunlight and warm temperatures to survive. Neither could thrive in the damp, cold environment of city sewers. The truth, however, rarely stops, or even slows, an urban legend. In fact, the more unlikely or unusual the story, the more people seem to enjoy repeating it. It certainly seems to make life more exciting for some to believe that alligators inhabit the sewers, cockroaches can hatch in a person's mouth, and a mouse can kill a buffalo. Or perhaps it is the simple joy of telling a story that keeps urban legends alive.

Albino alligators are said to lurk in the New York City sewer system. This legend has been in circulation for over seventy years.

Chapter 2

Food Fears and Fantasies

A ll humans have to eat to stay alive, and eating is among the few universal acts performed by people worldwide. But sometimes the food that is available harms people. In poorer nations, people are often sickened by contaminated food. In most industrialized nations, however, people are used to ingesting only foods, such as meats, sodas, and vegetables, that have been examined and approved by various government inspectors. Despite having access to one of the world's most hygienic food supplies, North Americans and Europeans continue to harbor age-old uncertainties about food. These qualms have spawned dozens of food-based urban legends in which incompetent food processors and malicious malefactors have tainted the very substances that sustain life. In some cases, however, fantasies and fears become nearly indistinguishable.

A Finger in the Chili

On March 22, 2005, a horror often propagated in urban legends became reality when a woman eating a bowl of chili at a Wendy's fast-food restaurant in San Jose, California, bit into a one-and-one-half-inch-long (3.81cm) piece of a woman's severed finger with a long, polished nail. Relatives of the diner who witnessed the discovery later told authorities that the woman had an extremely negative reaction. According to Ben Gale, director of the Department of Environmental

Health for Santa Clara County, "This individual apparently did take a spoonful, did have a finger in their mouth and then, you know, spit it out and recognized it. . . . Then they had some kind of emotional reaction and vomited."[17]

The story made headlines across the globe and became the subject of hundreds of late night talk show jokes. Business at all Wendy's restaurants across the nation plummeted, especially at the San Jose outlet. Within a month, the restaurant lost more than $2.5 million in business. Meanwhile, it was also reported that the woman who bit into the finger has a history of filing frivolous lawsuits, including one against another fast-food restaurant. When authorities theorized that the finger was purposely put into the chili by the woman, the diner declined to sue Wendy's.

While the nationally reported story of the finger in the chili was bizarre, it had an eerie resemblance to an urban legend

The San Jose police chief enjoys a bowl of Wendy's chili despite the claim of a woman to have found a severed finger in chili she bought at the restaurant a few months before.

that has been around since 1987. This story concerns two brothers from Southern California who were eating a bowl of canned menudo produced by a food processing company called Juanita's Farms. The brothers found a two-inch (5.08cm) piece of human finger, complete with fingernail, in their menudo. They dumped the food down the sink and took the finger to a hospital for analysis, where it was confirmed as human. According to the legend, police were called and they confiscated the finger, hoping to find its owner.

The urban legend developed from a harmless story into a serious problem when the news service United Press International wrote that the erroneous story was true. Unfortunately for Juanita's Farms, supermarkets quickly began disposing of thousands of cans of their menudo. The panicked executives of the company firmly stated that no accidents had taken place at the plant, so the finger was not in the menudo when it left the factory. However, over the next several months, Juanita's Farms lost about $1 million in sales. Relating this tale to the Wendy's story, an author identified only as Matthew on the SlashNot Web site writes:

> In a bizarre juxtaposition of coincidence, horror, and postmodern industrial lore, the "Human Finger in a Bowl of Chili" urban legend has accidentally come true. This particular urban legend has been told many ways but it usually involves meaty dark soups such as chili or menudo. The story is a member of an urban legend species with many variations, from mice and cockroaches in soda bottles to deep-fried rats served up in a bucket of chicken. But this particular urban legend turned to suburban horror earlier this week. [18]

In the weeks after Matthew's statement, the source of the finger at Wendy's remained a mystery. The diner's motives, however, proved to be more obvious. On April 22,

Anna Ayala is arraigned in a Las Vegas court after she was arrested on charges of fraud for claiming that she found a finger in her Wendy's chili.

2005, the woman was arrested and accused of planting the digit in the dinner herself, hoping to sue the restaurant. It remains unknown whether the fraudulent finger eater was inspired by the 1987 menudo legend. If so, she would not be the first person to mimic an urban legend. In fact, folk-lorist Linda Dégh invented the term *ostension* to describe the act of turning an urban legend into reality. In *Aliens, Ghosts, and Cults*, Bill Ellis explains:

> [The] ubiquity of information about such [urban legends] itself tends to influence irrational individuals to commit criminal acts. . . . Not every legend is based on some real event, nor does it have the ghoulish ability to compel one to enact the legend in real life. But the concept of ostension still helps explain

... ways in which circulating narratives can influence reality, or at least the way reality is interpreted.[19]

Fearsome Fruit and Contaminated Candy

A case of a legend that has permanently changed reality—and the behavior of an entire society—is the Razor Blades in Halloween Apples story. This legend has altered the way tens of millions of people celebrate Halloween and has cost society millions of dollars in useless actions to protect children from something that has rarely, if ever, happened.

Perhaps it should come as no surprise that one of the scariest urban legends is perpetuated on Halloween. However, the fear of tainted treats is a relatively new phenome-

Dining on Rats, Fingers, and Insects

There is no shortage of urban legends concerning contaminated food. However, as Jan Harold Brunvand writes in *The Choking Doberman and Other "New" Urban Legends*, the way people retell some stories often blurs the line between reality and urban legend:

"The Kentucky Fried Rat" [a deep-fried rat found in a bucket of KFC chicken] and "The Mouse in the Coke" are the best-known American food-contamination legends . . . along with some shuddering side glances at rumors of rat salads, wormburgers, spider-egg bubble gum, and other such nasties. . . . Exactly what portion of this kind of lore is genuinely folk may be debatable, since the news media regularly report contamination scares that are based on facts. . . . And people spread by word of mouth a complete mishmash of what they have read, what they have heard, and what they think they have read or heard.

In the past couple of years alone, for example, I have seen actual news stories quoting named individuals (usually the victims, their attorneys, or law-enforcement officers) describing a piece of human skin found in a can of Stokely-Van Camp tomato juice, and a live beetle found in a container of Dannon raspberry yogurt. I have been told stories about seeing a cockroach crawl out of a bowl of cream of tomato soup served in a restaurant, and of finding a chilled (but still living) snake in a package of frozen chitterlings. And at the furthest extreme of incredibility, I have heard vague rumors about a cigarette butt found in a Hershey chocolate bar, a dead mouse discovered in a box of Cheerios, a thumb frozen into a commercially sold ice cube, and . . . a gloved finger found in a jar of Progresso marinating sauce.

non. Until the late 1960s, those wishing to provide health-ier alternatives to sugary Halloween candy handed out ap-ples, oranges, or other fruits to trick-or-treaters. Today, that tradition has been universally abandoned. This comes as a result of a story that began circulating around 1967, in which an unnamed, deranged person put razor blades in ap-ples and handed them out to neighborhood children on Halloween. According to the story, children bit into the tainted apples and received serious cuts and lacerations. In the years that followed, the story was repeated and embell-ished every Halloween. The storytellers usually described the incident as having taken place close to their home, and the apples contained not only razor blades but also needles, poison, and even the hallucinogenic drug LSD. The legend also extended to poisoned or drugged candy.

The razor blade story changed the behavior of millions, who began to buy only individually wrapped candies to give away on Halloween. To counter fears of tainted candy, cities began sponsoring community events in which children could dress up and attend parties rather than trick-or-treat door-to-door. Getting into the act, hospitals across the na-tion began offering free X-rays for Halloween candy to as-sure parents the food was untainted by foreign objects. Within a few years, Halloween went from an innocent holi-day to a night fraught with danger.

The Razor in the Apple legend mysteriously created a national climate of fear based on a few isolated incidents. In 1985 researchers Joel Best and Gerald T. Horiuchi studied Halloween-related food contamination stories printed in newspapers. They found that between 1958 and 1984, only seventy-six incidents were reported, and most of them were Halloween hoaxes carried out by children who lied to scare their parents. While tens of millions of trick-or-treaters ex-perienced nothing more than stomachaches from gorging on candy, only a single person died as a result of contaminated

Urban legends about poisoned Halloween candy and razors hidden in fruit prey on the fear of parents that their children will fall victim to sadistic strangers.

food. And that eight-year-old boy, Timothy O'Bryan, was killed by his own father in a blatant case of ostension.

In a bizarre incident of an urban legend coming true, Ronald Clark O'Bryan of suburban Houston, Texas, laced a powdered candy called Pixie Stix with cyanide, a deadly poison. On Halloween night 1974, O'Bryan planted the tainted candy among the treats Timothy had collected. Timothy ate the candy and died; his father tried to collect a large insurance settlement using the poisoned candy legend as a cover. O'Bryan was arrested, convicted of murder, and executed in 1984. In *Perspectives on Contemporary Legend*, folklorist Sylvia Grider describes how the O'Bryan case, the media, and the Razor in the Apple legend blurred the line between food fears and reality:

> The media coverage of the crime has interacted with oral tradition and previous newspaper warnings, thus creating perhaps the most widespread Halloween

legend in America. The oral legend developed first, with infinite variety; then the media began annual isolated reports of tainted treats allegedly received by innocent children; then these reports were followed by terse warnings of the very real possibility that sadistic adults were preying on children at Halloween; and finally, the nightmare conclusion that a child was actually murdered with trick-or-treat candy. . . . That climax has now intensified the impact of the legend throughout the media and oral tradition because the murder is cited as proof and vindication of the warnings. The folklore component of this syndrome was never recognized by either the media or the law enforcement agencies; rather, the media took all previous reports of tainted treats and warnings as empirical truth and therefore linked all that had gone before with the O'Bryan murder. The legend was validated by the murder.[20]

Accidental Cannibalism

The O'Bryan murder helped bring about a climate of paranoia based on age-old fears of innocent children being preyed upon by sadistic strangers. The story has such staying power, however, because it is just plausible enough. Contaminated food legends have been disseminated for centuries and in many societies. More grisly than eating poison, some of the legends involve some sort of cannibalism.

One of the oldest contaminated food legends comes from fifteenth-century Italy. It involves a pair of Italian travelers in a foreign land. One man dies, and his friend wants to send the body home to Italy for burial. Unable to afford proper transport, the friend dismembers the body and pickles it in jars of spices and honey. But on the boat ride home, the jars are mistaken for exotic specialty food, and the contents are consumed by a Florentine businessman.

Whether the Italian Pickled Corpse legend had a basis in reality is unknown, but the legend took on a life of its own. In the following centuries, it mysteriously morphed into the English Corpse in the Cask legend, which itself has become a permanent part of English drinking culture. This story is based on reality. In the days before the widespread availability of embalming services, rich people such as diplomats, nobles, and wealthy traders who died in faraway places had their bodies preserved in a barrel of alcohol for shipment home. This practice was quickly linked to the notoriously hard-drinking sailors who worked on the ships, often for many months at sea. Legend has it that the sailors could not resist drilling small holes in the casks and sipping the alcohol through long straws.

Were There Ever Razors in Apples?

The story of razor blades in apples began to mysteriously appear in 1967. However, as Barbara Mikkelson and David P. Mikkelson write in the Web site Urban Legends Reference Pages, the stories covered in newspapers appear to be frauds that were never properly investigated:

The emergence of the [Razor Blades in Apples story] remains to be studied, but it apparently spread rapidly in several areas of the eastern seaboard and Canada: *The New York Times* reported thirteen cases. . . . Outrage was so strong in New Jersey that the state legislature passed a law shortly before Halloween 1968 mandating prison terms for those caught booby-trapping apples. This did not forestall the discovery of thirteen more apples with razor blades that year in five New Jersey counties.

In many cases, *The New York Times* story noted that "children were cut," but the more detailed accounts include suspicious details. In one case a boy came to his parents with an apple containing a razor blade. He had bit into an apple, he said, but not quite deeply enough to contact the blade. In another, the child said he found the blade while cutting out a rotten spot; in a third case, the razor was found when a child turned an apple over to his father for peeling. In all these detailed cases, the child was not injured, and because he was the immediate source of the apple, it seems possible that he was also the source of the blade. . . . [Virtually] all the reports were hoaxes concocted by the children or parents. Thus this legend . . . seems to have grown out of a tradition of . . . hoaxes . . . rather than on any core of authenticated incidents.

After British naval hero Horatio Nelson died in Spain, his body was preserved in a barrel of brandy, from which, according to legend, his shipmates drank.

This was said to be the case with the revered British naval hero Admiral Horatio Nelson. After his death in the Battle of Trafalgar, Spain, in 1805, his body was preserved in a barrel of brandy for shipment back to London. When it arrived, it was purportedly half full, giving rise to the phrase "tapping the admiral," [21] commonly used by British sailors to describe secretly drinking rum in defiance of a captain's orders.

An updated version of the story concerns cheap wine that is allegedly imported to Paris from Algeria in large tanker ships. After most of the wine is siphoned from the tanks and bottled, a dead Algerian with a knife in his back or a noose around his neck is found at the bottom of one of the shipping tanks.

"Cokelore"

The body-in-the-wine story proves that some urban legends, even those with roots in the Italian Renaissance or colonial England, mysteriously survive the test of time. Though the body goes from pickle jars to brandy barrels to modern tanker ships, the concept remains the same—something ghastly is found in the beverage. Tales about a drink consumed by millions of people across the globe every day may be the latest incarnation of this legend.

The Mouse in the Coca-Cola is a grotesque tale of someone who consumes a bottle or can of the popular soft drink only to find, variously, a decomposed mouse, parts of a mouse, or a mouse's tail in the container. Of course, the traumatized soda drinker sues and is rewarded a large sum of money.

This story is so common that it inspired urban legend researcher Gary Alan Fine of Northwestern University to trace it to its source. Fine examined thousands of state court records dating back decades and found that the Mouse in the Coke story was based on several real incidents. The first was a court case brought against Coca-Cola Bottling Company in Jackson, Mississippi, in 1914, when a man found a drowned mouse in his bottle of Coke. In the following years, forty-four more cases were found in twenty-three states and the District of Columbia. While lawsuits concerning frightening discoveries in Coke bottles were most prevalent, Fine also found cases involving several other tainted products like milk, beer, pies, and Chinese food. These contained a wide array of additional disgusting contaminants including cigarette butts, hairpins, condoms, and insects such as cockroaches, maggots, and worms.

Researchers speculate that some if not most of these cases are examples of ostension. People inspired by urban legends are purposefully polluting foods in order to sue the manufacturers. Whatever the case, folklore specifically concerning the Mouse in the Coke is so common that Fine coined the term "Cokelore"[22] to refer to it.

The mouse story is just one example of Cokelore. Another tale that has circulated for decades states that combin-

Dangerous Beliefs About Mountain Dew

Mountain Dew soda, made by PepsiCo, is laden with large servings of sugar and caffeine. While these ingredients may cause drinkers to be hyperactive and nervous, there is nothing in Mountain Dew that acts as birth control. This unfortunate legend, however, seems to have originated in Michigan in the late 1990s, quickly spreading across the country. In *The Complete Idiot's Guide to Urban Legends*, Brandon Toropov examines some possible consequences from this mysterious story:

> This is one of those legends that's not merely false, but also more than a little unsettling. Suppose that teenagers and young adults across the country actually started believing that swigging down Mountain Dew made it unlikely or impossible to impregnate one's

partner? Well, that's what high school and college kids across the country began telling each other in late 1999.

Will unplanned pregnancies skyrocket in communities with high concentrations of Dew drinkers? We're still monitoring the data. But using soda for birth control is a pretty dumb idea, no matter how you analyze it.

Here's another question: Could fears regarding the onset of adult sexuality, combined with easy Internet access, have some role in the popularity of such stories? It's a theory. The only thing that the people at PepsiCo are sure of is that they didn't mean for the stuff to be used as birth control.

ing Coca-Cola and aspirin has many incredible effects. It is said to variously get the drinker high, act as an aphrodisiac, or even cause instant death. This story originated in the 1930s when a doctor writing to the American Medical Association allegedly warned teenagers against dissolving aspirin in Coke because it would have a narcotic effect. While totally false, people have mysteriously managed to keep this story alive for decades as many people have choked down Coke and melted aspirin, hoping to get a cheap high.

Another category of Cokelore relates to the alleged hazardous qualities of the ingredients. Coca-Cola, along with many other soft drinks, contains phosphoric acid. This gave rise to the notion that a tooth, iron nail, or even a T-bone steak would dissolve if left in a cup of Coke overnight. However, the amount of phosphoric acid is so small, about one-fifth of 1 percent, that it will not liquefy iron, teeth, or meat in a short amount of time. Coke could dissolve these items over an extended period of time but so can many of the other substances people commonly ingest, including orange juice.

This fact did little to stop the e-mail alert that circulated in recent years with the subject line reading "Say Bye to Coke!!"[23] This e-mail stated that Coke contains phosphoric acid. But even worse, the writer warned, Coke contains ethylene glycol, the main ingredient in automobile antifreeze. This substance, which prevents water from freezing in car radiators when the temperature dips below zero, is extremely toxic. The warning concludes: "So, if you manage to drink about 4 liters of Coke within an hour or so, you can die."[24]

The author of this e-mail mysteriously ignores an obvious fact: If someone could die from drinking that much

So many urban legends about Coca-Cola have been generated over the years that an urban folklorist coined the term "Cokelore" to refer to them collectively.

Coke, dozens of deaths would be reported in the media. What the author of this urban legend did was twist some facts to come to an unproven, if not irrational, conclusion. Coke contains propylene glycol, not ethylene glycol. While both substances are used in antifreeze, and can kill in high doses, the amount of the chemical in Coke is so minuscule that it is harmless. According to the Centers for Disease Control (CDC): "The Food and Drug Administration (FDA) has classified propylene glycol as an additive that is 'generally recognized as safe' for use in food. It is used to absorb extra water and maintain moisture in certain medicines, cosmetics, or food products."[25]

While few would claim that drinking large quantities of soda is good for a person, people have little to fear from the trace amounts of propylene glycol found in Coke.

"No Beaks, No Feathers, and No Feet"

While some food legends are based on faulty science, others are completely bizarre. One wacky legend began circulating on the Internet around 1999 as a neatly typed e-mail marked "Boycott KFC." The e-mail stated that the fast-food chain Kentucky Fried Chicken changed its name to KFC because the restaurant no longer served chicken. To prove the point, the e-mail writer quoted a study allegedly conducted by the University of New Hampshire:

> The reason why they call it KFC is because they can not use the word chicken anymore. Why? KFC does not use real chickens. They actually use genetically manipulated organisms. These so called "chickens" are kept alive by tubes inserted into their bodies to pump blood and nutrients throughout their structure. They have no beaks, no feathers, and no feet. Their bone structure is dramatically shrunk to get more meat out of them. This is great for KFC

because they do not have to pay so much for their production costs. There is no more plucking of the feathers or the removal of the beaks and feet.

The government has told them to change all of their menus so they do not say chicken anywhere. If you look closely you will notice this. Listen to their commercials, I guarantee you will not see or hear the word chicken. I find this matter to be very disturbing. I hope people will start to realize this and let other people know.

Please forward this message to as many people as you can. Together we make KFC start using real chicken again.[26]

Although KFC changed its name in 1991, eight years before the e-mail, thousands of people inexplicably believed the mutant chicken rumor. Colette Janson-Sand, associate professor of nutrition at the University of New Hampshire, where the study was said to be conducted, says her department received hundreds of phone calls, some that were described as "hysterical." The university stated on its Web site that "there is no such research or study that was done here."[27] Enough people were concerned about the issue, however, that the Web site received over five thousand hits daily after the e-mail began to circulate. The university explained the possible reasons people wanted to believe the urban legend:

It starts with a well known subject (KFC) and a timely topic (genetic modification of animals and plants) and then spins out a story that progresses from possible, to improbable, and finally to impossible. As an extra touch of false verisimilitude [believability], there is the vague reference to a study at the University of New Hampshire![28]

The Web site touches on common fears people have of transgenic food crops, which some call Frankenfoods after the legendary monster pieced together by Dr. Frankenstein from several different humans. The story runs into trouble, however, by claiming that the company raises its own chickens. KFC is a restaurant and buys chickens from hundreds of suppliers across the globe. There is no single KFC chicken farm where the 800 million chickens that the company uses each year are raised. In addition, common sense would indicate that the company took the word "fried" out of its name because of the unhealthy image many people have about fried food.

Whatever the case, the KFC story shares common traits with other legends. According to Brandon Toropov in *The Complete Idiot's Guide to Urban Legends*, some are told from the point of view that "the big corporation is out to get you,"[29] while others highlight supposed government inadequacy. In this case, hundreds of millions of people are being fed monster chickens and all the government can do is ask the company not to use the word *chicken* in its name.

Although KFC's menu makes it clear the restaurant serves bona fide chicken, many people continue to believe the myth that the company uses a chicken substitute.

Although a quick visit to KFC would prove that the company does use the word *chicken* on its menu, the far-reaching consequences of the Chicken That Isn't Chicken story shows that even a bogus story can be given serious consideration when posted on the Internet.

Long before the invention of e-mail, renowned author Mark Twain said, "A lie can travel halfway around the world while the truth is putting on its shoes." [30] However, it remains a mystery to researchers how the lies about KFC, Coke, and dozens of other urban legends can be taken so seriously by so many people. But the fact remains, an urban legend can travel around the world in minutes while the truth, bafflingly, takes much more time and effort to transmit.

Chapter 3

Government Conspiracies

Many people believe that politicians and government bureaucrats stretch the truth and cover up a wide array of illicit acts. A quick check of best-seller lists over the years will reveal hundreds of books that have exposed distortions, exaggerations, and fabrications by government officials ranging from small-town mayors to presidents of the United States. Other books reveal questionable actions taken by government agencies such as the Internal Revenue Service (IRS), the Central Intelligence Agency (CIA), and even the National Aeronautics and Space Administration (NASA).

Whether or not the writers of these books have their own agenda, the fact is millions of Americans do not trust their government. And the trust has deteriorated over the years. A *Washington Post* poll shows that in 1964, 75 percent of Americans trusted the government to do the right thing; by 1994 that number had sunk to 20 percent. While the numbers of people who trust their government has gone up since that low more than a decade ago, according to a 2004 *New York Times*/CBS News poll, two out of three Americans stated that they did not necessarily believe what the government told them.

Over the years, widespread distrust of the government has led to a virtual industry in urban legends about government conspiracies. Hundreds of books, magazine articles, and Web pages have been written about the government's

role in covering up what "really" happened in dozens of incidents. As Gary Alan Fine and Patricia A. Turner write in
Whispers on the Color Line,

> Allegations persisted that the official explanations for
> the deaths of John F. Kennedy and Martin Luther
> King, Jr. were false. Rumors suggested a government

*In 1995 rescue workers
make their way inside the
bombed out Oklahoma
City Federal Building to
search for survivors. The
bombing spawned several
government conspiracy
rumors.*

conspiracy in the bombings of the Oklahoma City Federal Building [in April 1995] and the Olympic Park in Atlanta [in 1996]. . . . Those who report these rumors frequently identify "the government" or one particular agency as the evil perpetrator. . . . Mistrust of government is long-standing and endemic.[31]

Flying Saucers in New Mexico

Clearly, mysterious circumstances surround many of these alleged government conspiracies. The federal government operates a host of top-secret civilian and military agencies that carry out hundreds of covert missions. Such programs are often unknown to anyone except a few high-level officials and the president. If the public accidentally discovers some information about secret missions, urban legends can spin out of control. This seems to be the case with the alleged UFO sightings in Roswell, New Mexico, in the late forties.

The incident began on July 5, 1947, when Mac Brazel, a rancher who lived near the remote town of Roswell, New Mexico, found some strange-looking debris in his pasture. He described the wreckage as consisting of a foil-like substance of unearthly strength inscribed with strange symbols resembling hieroglyphics. Brazel also said he found beams made of material resembling balsa wood and a strange sort of string. The next day, the rancher transported pieces of the debris to the offices of the local sheriff, who notified intelligence officers at the nearby military base, Roswell Air Army Field. Military officials picked up the debris and carted it away for analysis. The next day, according to the *Roswell Daily Record*, the air force issued an official statement saying it was in possession of "a flying saucer."[32] Several hours later, Brigadier General Roger Ramey retracted the first statement and said that the debris came from a weather balloon.

At the time of Brazel's discoveries, the country was going through what has been described as UFO mania. Two

Government officials examine bits of a weather balloon that started rumors that an alien spacecraft crashed in Roswell, New Mexico, in 1947.

weeks earlier, businessman Kenneth Arnold was flying a private plane near Mount Rainier in Washington when he allegedly saw nine boomerang-shaped, glowing objects hurtling across the sky at incredible speed. Arnold went to the press and said the objects were moving erratically, as "a saucer would if you skipped it across water."[33] When the story went out on the wire services, the objects were described as "flying saucers." This was the first time the term was ever used, and an urban legend was born. People immediately associated Arnold's sighting with space aliens and UFOs.

Between Belief and Disbelief

UFO mania has been blamed on the frenzy that followed the "Roswell Incident." Some speculate that the air force

Doctored images, like this 1963 photo, convince many that UFOs are real and that the government has orchestrated a conspiracy to hide their existence.

official who said the Roswell debris was from a flying saucer was caught up in the hysteria. Others speculate that the material in Brazel's pasture had been lying there for nearly a month, and the rancher was only prompted to report it after he too was swept up in the panic. Whatever the case, in the years that followed, hundreds of UFO sightings were reported from thirty-two states and Canada. Many were sensationalized in the press, and each spawned its own urban legend. The Web page article "The Grand Conspiracy" lists some of these alleged sightings:

> In July of 1952, a panicked government watched helplessly as squadrons of flying saucers flew over Washington, D.C., and buzzed the White House, the Capitol Building, and the Pentagon. It took all the imagination and intimidation the government could muster to force that incident out of the memory of the public. Thousands of sightings occurred during the Korean War [1950–1953] and several more saucers were retrieved by the Air Force. Some were stored at Wright Patterson Air Force Base [in Ohio]; some were stored at Air Force bases near the locations of the crash sites. One saucer was so enormous and the logistics problems in transporting it so great that it was buried at the crash site and remains there today.[34]

Such urban legends prompted the air force to expend great effort to prove that all UFO sightings were attributed to natural phenomena such as northern lights, meteors, and swamp gas. The military went further, encouraging friendly reporters in the national media to write articles that labeled believers in flying saucers as unreliable eccentrics.

Mysteriously, the more the air force tried to dissuade people from believing in aliens, the more people seemed to believe in them. Belief in flying saucers and space aliens grew

Elements of Government Legends

Many people who believe dire conspiracy theories often share an element of paranoia and fear concerning the government, as Brandon Toropov writes in *The Complete Idiot's Guide to Urban Legends:*

> The government is not the network of inept, shortsighted bureaucrats that it may seem to be from a distance. It is actually a powerful, many-tentacled monster that's basically out to get you (or keep you from discovering the truth).
>
> This many-tentacled monster is ominously withholding (or is about to withhold) something essential to humanity (access to spe-cial knowledge or documents, access to the Internet, access to new technologies, the ability to exercise fundamental rights, and so on).
>
> Thanks to the selfless efforts of those select few who are "in the know" (self-appointed "researchers," activists, persecuted innocents, witnesses of alien autopsies, and so on), this monster can be overcome through a grass-roots informational effort. Such an effort ensures (at some point in the not-too-distant future) . . . humanity's eventual inheritance of [the essential knowledge, documents, or inventions that] it had coming all along.

Conspiracy paranoia is expressed in this cartoon that portrays the government as a faceless giant pursuing a terrified individual.

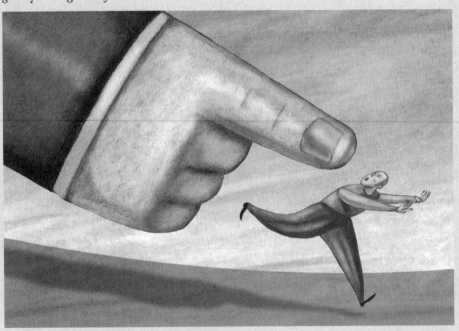

each decade. By the 1970s, hundreds of urban legends had sprung forth from the Roswell Incident, many fueled by the growing number of books and television programs about the issue. In one legend, it was said that two four-foot-tall (1.22m) space aliens were found among the Roswell wreckage. They looked like preying mantises and were much more intellectually advanced than human beings. These creatures were supposedly spirited away by shadowy military personnel who conducted autopsies on them. It was said that other aliens came to rescue those who crashed at Roswell and, according to "The Grand Conspiracy,"

> On April 30, 1964, the first communication between these aliens and the U.S. Government took place at Holloman Air Force base in New Mexico. Three saucers landed at a pre-arranged area and a meeting was held between the aliens and intelligence officers of the U.S. Government. During the period between 1969 to 1971, [representatives of] the U.S. Government, made a deal with these creatures. . . . The "deal" was that in exchange for "technology" that they would provide us, we agreed to "ignore" the [alien] abductions that were going on. . . . [The aliens assured the government] that the abductions (usually lasting about two hours) were merely the ongoing monitoring of developing civilizations. [35]

However bizarre such legends seemed to skeptics, they fueled the belief that the government was engaged in a conspiracy to cover up the existence of extraterrestrials. In 1997, on the fiftieth anniversary of the Roswell sighting, a CNN/*Time* poll showed that 80 percent of Americans continued to believe that the government was hiding knowledge of the existence of extraterrestrial life forms. Whether the believers are right, or whether the rumors of aliens and flying saucers are simply urban legends, will likely never be known. As David Emery writes in the Web article "Roswell: Birth of a Legend,"

> The facts [concerning the Roswell Incident] have become so obscured by a half-century of mythologizing that not even the mainstream press can differentiate between the truth and hearsay of it anymore.
>
> In the public mind, Roswell now occupies [a] curious limbo between belief and disbelief. . . . [We've] been assaulted with so much contradictory information from so many quarters that it no longer seems reasonable to expect we'll ever know what really happened.[36]

The Death of a President

The flying saucer incidents of the 1950s did not immediately fuel a widespread distrust in the government. In fact, in the early sixties, public trust in elected officials and federal agencies was at an all-time high. For many, however, that trust was shattered soon after November 22, 1963, the day President John F. Kennedy was assassinated in Dallas, Texas. Kennedy was shot while driving in an open convertible in broad daylight in front of thousands of people lining a parade route in Dallas. However, this happened in an era before quality point-and-shoot cameras, video cameras, portable tape recorders, cell phones, and twenty-four-hour news coverage. A single grainy film strip shot with a cheap movie camera—with no audio—is the only known historic record of that tragedy.

The alleged murderer, Lee Harvey Oswald, was himself shot to death two days later—while in police custody—by a strip club owner named Jack Ruby. The only time the public got to hear Oswald's side of the story was after the murder, as police marched him into jail, where he proclaimed loudly to the assembled press that he was a patsy, that is, a person who was deliberately set up to take the blame for—

and divert attention from—the real killer or killers. Despite the denial, the government's official investigation of the assassination later pinned the blame on Oswald, saying that he was a crazed lone gunman with a grudge against the president. Thus began one of the longest-running mysteries in American history—and an event that spawned countless urban legends.

In the immediate aftermath of the murder, millions of Americans came to believe that Oswald was an agent working for the Communist Soviet Union, an enemy of the United States at that time. Based on this myth, some were

One of the most persistent urban legends concerns a conspiracy surrounding the assassination of John F. Kennedy in 1963.

55

Moments after this photo was taken, Kennedy's assassin, Lee Harvey Oswald (center), was shot and killed by Jack Ruby, who some people say was hired to cover up a conspiracy.

calling for immediate war with the Soviet Union, something that might have led to total nuclear destruction of the planet. However, the new president, Lyndon Johnson, quickly quashed that urban legend after discussing the assassination with the Soviet leadership.

By that time, Oswald had been captured and killed, and the media had begun to look into the mysterious life of the al-

leged assassin. Investigators soon discovered that in his short life, the twenty-four-year-old Oswald had made various contacts with the FBI, the CIA, the Mafia, and right-wing Cuban exiles who hated Kennedy. These discoveries spawned a widespread distrust in the government's version of events.

Only one year after Kennedy's death, a Gallup poll showed that over 50 percent of Americans believed that the contradictions and confounding facts behind Kennedy's assassination proved a high-level conspiracy—and that his murderers had gone unpunished. As millions of Americans joined the ranks of conspiracy theorists, urban legends were put forth stating that Kennedy was killed by a shadowy group of men who had connections variously to the Mafia, the FBI, Texas oilmen, Cuban refugees, the Ku Klux Klan, the man who took over Kennedy's job, Lyndon Baines Johnson, or even the man Kennedy defeated in the previous election, Richard M. Nixon. In later years, when the Vietnam War escalated into a bloody conflict, it was said Kennedy was killed by a group of defense contractors and generals because he did not want to fight the war. Each legend has its believers, witnesses, and those who swear they were there.

In the years after the Kennedy assassination, dozens of books appeared in print that called nearly every detail of the government version of events into question. (Today over six hundred have been written about the event.) These books have created a tangled web of interlocking urban legends, some plausible and some inexplicable.

As the number of urban legends increased, politicians, writers, and mainstream magazines such as *Life* and *Newsweek* tried to debunk the various theories. Over the years, however, these efforts have had little apparent effect. In 2003, on the fortieth anniversary of the assassination, a Gallup poll showed that more than 75 percent of Americans believed that more than one person was involved in the shooting of the president.

As with the Roswell Incident, the president's murder created a virtual urban legend industry based on government distrust. Rumor theorist Ralph Rosnow explains:

> John Kennedy's assassination produced a spate of [urban legends], many still alive in the hearts and minds of those disinclined to believe the [government's version of events]. Leaving aside the justification of these [legends], it is not unreasonable to forecast that one hundred years from now stories will still be circulating about that fateful November day. [37]

The Government and AIDS

Urban legends that linked the Central Intelligence Agency and the Federal Bureau of Investigation to the Kennedy assassination shocked millions of white Americans, regardless of their political background. However, the alleged deeds of the CIA and the FBI often play a large role in the government-based urban legends that circulate in African American communities. Perhaps it is because agents working for the FBI have been traced to various campaigns against black leaders. For example, according to a 1976 report written by the U.S. Senate Select Committee in Intelligence called "Intelligence Activities and the Rights of Americans,"

> From late 1963 until his death in 1968, Martin Luther King, Jr., was the target of an intensive campaign by the Federal Bureau of Investigation to "neutralize" him as an effective civil rights leader. In the words of the man in charge of the FBI's "war" against Dr. King, "No holds were barred." . . . The FBI gathered information about Dr. King's plans and activities through an extensive surveillance program, employing nearly every intelligence-gathering technique at the Bureau's disposal in order to obtain information about the "private activities of Dr. King

and his advisors" to use to "completely discredit" them. . . . In early 1968, Bureau headquarters explained to the field [agents] that Dr. King must be destroyed because he was seen as a potential "messiah" who could "unify and electrify" the "black nationalist movement."[38]

While the harassment of the civil rights leader was verified by previously secret FBI files, the bureau has never been

The FBI spied on Martin Luther King Jr. for years, leading many to speculate that the agency had a hand in his 1968 murder.

legally linked to King's 1968 assassination in Memphis, Tennessee. However, after he was murdered, rumors immediately swept through dozens of black communities in America that the government was responsible for his death. Although it is unknown if this legend contributed to the violence, deadly riots quickly erupted in black communities in large cities throughout the country. In the aftermath, even without specific evidence, a substantial number of people continued to believe that King was killed by an agent or agents working for the government.

With such a widespread distrust of the government, perhaps it is not surprising that many blame the government for spreading AIDS in black communities. When AIDS first appeared in the early 1980s, it primarily affected the gay community. Before long, however, researchers discovered that the virus was also infecting a disproportionate number of African Americans and black Haitian and African immigrants. Spotting a trend, the media began notifying the public with headlines such as "Special Help Needed to Halt Black AIDS Cases," "AIDS More Prevalent Among Black Military Recruits," and the sensationalistic "Black Man's Teeth a Deadly Weapon, Jury Rules."[39]

At the time, much less was known about AIDS, and the general public had little understanding of why one group might be at a higher risk than another. In this situation, people invented their own theories about the origin of AIDS, and many of them are most likely urban legends. In 1987 Patricia A. Turner, a professor of African American studies, conducted her own research to discover what black people thought of the origins of the AIDS epidemic. After talking to several hundred people who were average workers, students, professionals, and military personnel, she found that many people believed the disease to be a government conspiracy directed against blacks. Turner describes her findings in *I Heard It Through the Grapevine:*

A Basis for Belief?

Many urban legends about government conspiracies have little basis in reality. However, there have been instances of real conspiracies by government agents that might have been considered urban legends at the time they were carried out. For example, in the 1960s, the FBI and other government agencies tried to undermine members of the antiwar and civil rights movements. These actions helped fuel a virtual industry of urban legends concerning government conspiracies. A 1976 report by the U.S. Senate called "Intelligence Activities and the Rights of Americans" describes some of the activities actually undertaken by FBI agents:

Anonymously attacking the political beliefs of targets in order to induce their employers to fire them;

Anonymously mailing letters to the spouses of intelligence targets for the purpose of destroying their marriages;

Obtaining from IRS the tax returns of a target and then attempting to provoke an IRS investigation for the express purpose of deterring a protest leader from attending the [1968] Democratic National Convention;

Falsely and anonymously labeling as Government informants members of groups known to be violent, thereby exposing the falsely labeled member to expulsion or physical attack;

Pursuant to instructions to use "misinformation" to disrupt demonstrations, employing such means as broadcasting fake orders on the same citizens band radio frequency used by demonstration marshals to attempt to control demonstrations. . . .

Several motifs recur frequently. (1) Some branch of the U.S. government is usually the author of the conspiracy (informants have identified the CIA, the army, the Reagan administration, the Pentagon, the Centers for Disease Control, the far right, and "the superpowers"). . . . (2) The contamination targets of the conspiracy are labeled as Africans or descendants of Africans, either directly or by implication—for example, Haitians, Africans, blacks, black babies, the lower classes, and the outcasts of society. . . . (3) The conspiracy is described usually as either an experiment or as the intentional use of biological/chemical/germ warfare; hence, the goal is either to learn more about an experimental weapon or actually to use a known weapon against a targeted group. (4) The spread of the disease through groups other than those intended by the conspirators (such as white heterosexuals) is cited as a big mistake made by those in charge when the disease became too powerful for them. (5) . . . [The] informant will make the familiar comment, "I know it's true, I read it in the paper/saw it on television"— identified in folklore shorthand as r.i.p. (read it in paper).[40]

Urban legends about AIDS blame government agencies for inventing the disease in a lab as a weapon to use against minority groups like African Americans.

Turner's research shows similar beliefs across a broad cross section of the black population. In the 1990s several polls were taken on the subject. A *New York Times*/CBS

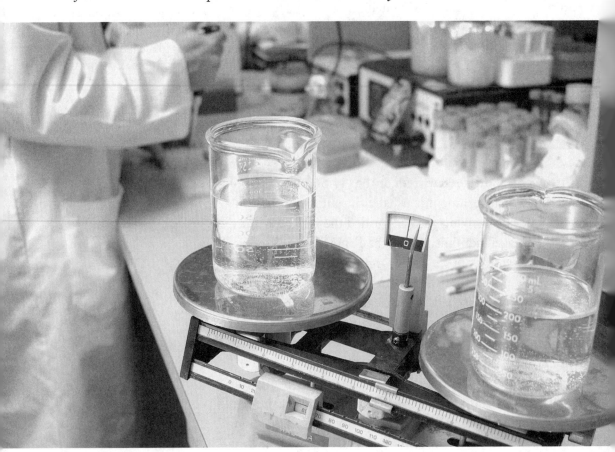

News poll showed that 29 percent of black respondents agreed that "the virus which causes AIDS was deliberately created in a laboratory to infect black people."[41] By comparison, only 1 to 4 percent of white people held these views.

"A White Man's Plot"

Although the true origin of AIDS is unknown, many scientists believe that the disease started in African chimpanzees and somehow transferred to humans, possibly through the ingestion of tainted monkey meat. Despite this theory, manifestations of AIDS urban legends proliferate. Some claim that the CIA was testing AIDS on blacks to see if it could be developed as a weapon, but the experiment got out of control. Since the disease was worse among black Haitians, a rumor started that the government deliberately infected people of that country to prevent them from immigrating to the United States.

Like many urban legends that allege government conspiracies, the CIA/AIDS stories are impossible to prove or disprove. If an experiment that got out of hand really existed, most people find it difficult to imagine the CIA admitting the truth. In addition, various government agencies actually do work to create, study, and weaponize deadly diseases such as small pox. Whether or not the AIDS story is an urban legend, some easily equate the creation of chemical and biological weapons to the unleashing of a sexually transmitted virus on an unsuspecting public.

Whatever the case, like many government conspiracy urban legends, the AIDS stories can have dangerous repercussions. Some studies have shown that people who believe the government is spreading AIDS feel that there is nothing they can do to stop the disease. This feeling of powerlessness makes some people less likely to practice safe sex, get AIDS tests, or take other measures to protect themselves. As Fine and Turner write:

Official Denial

In 1987, urban legend researcher Patricia A. Turner discovered that about one-third of black people believe the story that the CIA was originally responsible for starting the AIDS epidemic in order to wipe out African Americans. In response to this rumor, Turner sent an inquiry to the CIA. A spokesman wrote back, saying that the CIA was not responsible, and then tried to start what just might be another urban legend—that the Soviet Union was spreading the rumor to harm the U.S. government. The CIA letter is reprinted in Turner's *I Heard It Through the Grapevine:*

We believe that rumors linking the CIA with the development or the spreading of the AIDS virus . . . may be the result of what we would call "disinformation" efforts of hostile intelligence services to damage the United States. The CIA has had absolutely nothing to do with either the development or the spreading of AIDS or any other virus. The CIA is not carrying out experiments in this regard and you may document this by corresponding with either the House or Senate Select Committees on Intelligence which monitor Agency operations. The CIA has undertaken to try to understand the effects of the AIDS virus around the world, since it is clear that the spreading of such a disease could constitute a threat to US national security.

People dismiss their personal risk and blame it on the machinations of others, discounting the credibility of health care workers who attempt to protect minority communities. Indeed, the proposal to use condoms is attributed to government attempts to push minority population control. . . . Some African Americans with HIV believe that the medication AZT actually speeds up their symptoms and refuse to take the drug. [42]

With such attitudes, some believe that the unproved urban legends might be hastening the spread of AIDS. As Dr. Beni Primm, an African American and former member of the government's Commission on AIDS, states: "If I had as many people out there pushing the combat against AIDS as I have pushing the notion that it's a white man's plot, we would be winning the battle." [43]

The AIDS legends are among the darkest concerning government malfeasance. Whether the narrators of such stories actually believe them remains unknown. However, as long as officials cover up mistakes and generate reams of classified materials, creators of urban legends will continue to mistrust the government. And those suspicions will continue to circulate in conspiracy-based urban legends.

Chapter 4

Legends of Stage and Screen

I n the modern world, celebrities are constantly in the public eye. While movie stars, rock musicians, and other famous people are showered with adoration and money, there
is a dark side to celebrity. Every personal detail of their lives
is open for discussion, analysis, and rumor, most often by
people they never met. For example, when *Friends* star Jennifer Aniston and movie star Brad Pitt were separated in
2005, gossip, lies, and innuendo about their marriage—and
its failure—appeared in print in magazines across the globe.
Unflattering pictures, speculation by experts, and outright
lies appeared on countless television shows and on thousands
of Web sites and Internet discussion boards. Tellers of urban
legends speculated, among other things, that Aniston was
not interested in having a child with Pitt and that Pitt was
involved with a different actress or even dozens of actresses.

However painful this situation might be for celebrities
like Pitt and Aniston, it is widely believed that people trade
their privacy for the riches and fame of stardom. As Richard
Roeper writes in *Hollywood Urban Legends,*

> It's the first rule of celebrity life: The moment you
> become famous is the moment when people start

telling lies about you. Ninety-nine percent of these rumormongers will never meet you, never have a conversation with you, never be wronged by you, never have any reason to spread untruths about you —but that won't matter. What matters is, you belong to the world, and the world is filled with people who love to spread salacious tales about people in the public eye, whether those stories have any basis in fact or not. After all, you're not a flesh-and-blood human being with feelings; you're a celebrity, and this is part of the trade-off. If you didn't want to be the target of such stories, why didn't you stay in

The breakup of Jennifer Aniston and Brad Pitt in 2005 became instant grist for rumor mills around the world.

your hometown and find work as a forklift operator or a receptionist?[44]

While rumors and urban legends are most often spread by those who never actually met the celebrity in question, people seem ready to accept even the most bizarre stories about the rich and famous. Perhaps this is because urban legends often mix what is familiar with that which is dark and unknown. This is nowhere better demonstrated than by the legends spread about the most clean-cut characters from the early days of television.

The End of Innocence

The show *Leave It to Beaver* is synonymous with the innocence of life in America in the late 1950s. In this program about the perfect suburban family, the father, Ward Cleaver, always wore a tie to dinner, and mother June was always perfectly composed and in control. The show revolved around the young boy, Beaver, whose most serious offense was telling white lies to cover up minor mistakes.

By the mid-1960s, however, many Americans had lost their innocence. The assassination of Kennedy, the widespread use of drugs, the Vietnam War, and violent antiwar and civil rights protests made the trials and tribulations of Beaver seem laughably antiquated only a few years after the show went off the air in 1963. Conceivably this is why *Leave It to Beaver* became the subject of several dark urban legends by the late sixties.

One legend of mysterious origins stated that Jerry Mathers, the child actor who played Beaver, had grown up, joined the army, and was killed in Vietnam. Mikkelson and Mikkelson analyze the possible reasons this strange legend was circulated:

> *Leave It to Beaver* and its young star were seen as the tangible representations of a time of peaceful inno-

cence that ended not long after the show aired its final episode in September 1963. . . . Urban legends frequently juxtapose concepts such as good and evil, innocence and depravity, safety and danger, and what could provide a more shocking contrast in opposites than the announcement that one of our best known symbols of innocence and purity had met a violent death in a controversial war? . . . An actor who had been highly visible on TV every week for six years suddenly disappeared from the sight of the public eye, he was the same age as thousands of young men who were being drafted into the military and shipped overseas to fight in Vietnam, and the notion of his dying a soldier's death would be an ironic commentary on the social and political decline of America.[45]

In reality, Mathers did try to join the marines. However, he was told that he could not go to Vietnam because his possible death would have reflected negatively on the war effort.

J. Lo's Tale

Some celebrities love urban legends because the stories keep their name in the news and are often good for their careers. Perhaps this is why Jennifer Lopez, or J. Lo, as she is often called, was very coy when a legend surfaced about her insuring a specific part of her anatomy. David Emery explains on the Urban Legends and Folklore Web site:

[No] celebrity body part in recent memory has achieved greater prominence than J. Lo's derriere. . . . There's no getting around it, Jennifer Lopez's personal fame has very nearly been eclipsed by that of her own behind.

Nor is there any getting around rampant rumors of a comparably deluxe insurance policy. In 1999, tabloids on both sides of the Atlantic—*The Sun* in London and the *New York Post*—ran articles claiming that Jennifer Lopez had indemnified her body (her entire body, please note) to the tune of $1 billion. [However], word on the street soon had it that the "abundant butt" alone was valued at a cool billion.

Lopez [offered unclear or conflicting information when asked about the story].

"I don't know where they got it from. . . . When I heard the story I thought it was very funny."

Her agent's response was even more vague: "At this time we cannot confirm or deny this information." . . .

The closest to a straightforward disavowal I've found in print appeared in an August 2000 interview . . . in which she was asked to name the "wildest rumors" she had heard about herself.

"The craziest," she said, "was the Billion Dollar Butt one. . . . It was funny."

The interviewer pressed on: "So you haven't insured your body?"

"I think that's what I'm trying to say here," Lopez replied.

Draw your own conclusion

Instead Mathers served in the National Guard. Although he never left American soil during the war, Mather's military service gave rise to an urban legend that endures to this day.

Mr. Rogers Rumors

Child actors, probably because of their perceived innocence, are often the subject of urban legends. For the same reason, hosts of children's television shows also generate their fair share of myths. And few are as charming as Fred Rogers, the smiling, friendly host of *Mr. Rogers' Neighborhood*, a beloved children's show that first appeared on PBS in 1968.

Perhaps no TV star was more familiar and more comforting to the millions of children who grew up watching *Mr. Rogers' Neighborhood*. The host, in his fuzzy sweater and comfortable shoes, taught children to love, respect, and be kind to one another. There were those, however, who could not believe that such a nice man truly existed. These people, unnamed and unknown, began to circulate an urban legend that the man behind the cardigan was hiding some sinister secrets and was, in reality, the opposite of the person he portrayed on television.

In the late 1990s, it was said that Fred Rogers was a sharpshooter who killed dozens of people when he served in the army during the Vietnam War. The sweaters he wore allegedly covered dozens of shocking tattoos on his arms. If the image of Mr. Rogers shooting people in the head was not troubling enough, another legend, which began circulating around the same time, said Rogers was a convicted child molester. As part of his sentence, he was ordered to perform community service by appearing on a children's television show.

Such disturbing rumors have no basis in fact, and anyone who cared to research the background of Fred Rogers would discover that he had been in the television business since the 1950s. Rogers was a producer of several well-known shows

The sweet, gentle persona of Mr. Rogers inspired cynical stories that the host of the children's TV show had a hidden, dark past.

until he began developing a children's show for what would become PBS in 1963. The man was never in the military and, in fact, attended Pittsburgh Theological Seminary in the early sixties; he also served as a Presbyterian minister throughout the decade.

Muppet Myths

While Fred Rogers was undoubtedly hurt by the urban legends that people told about him, others at the center of persistent myths are less likely to complain. That is because, while they are comforting and familiar characters, they are not humans but fuzzy puppets called Muppets. Such is the case of Ernie, the beloved star of *Sesame Street*.

The Muppet myths began in 1990 when the creator of *Sesame Street*, Jim Henson, died suddenly of pneumonia. Henson was the voice of Ernie, and the combination of death and innocence proved to be too tempting to those who spread urban legends. Before long, people were saying that Ernie was going to die on the show. It was surmised that no one else could provide Ernie with his voice or, alternatively, that the show's producers, Jim Henson Productions and the Children's Television Workshop (CTW), wanted to teach children about death.

Hundreds of calls poured into the offices of the Children's Television Workshop, and the staff was stretched thin assuring troubled parents that Ernie was going to be kept alive as soon as a new actor could be found to provide his voice. Despite the producer's promises, the story took on a life of its own. Storytellers embellished the urban legend with new ways that the Muppet would meet his death. Listeners heard that Ernie would die of cancer, AIDS, and leukemia. Others heard speculations that the character would be gruesomely squashed under the wheels of a truck, bus, or automobile.

"They Are Puppets, Not Humans"

Ernie's sidekick, Bert, soon became associated with another Muppets urban legend. Not only was Bert alleged to die the same ways as Ernie, but it was said that the character had to be killed because of the erroneous belief that the man who acted as Bert's voice died of AIDS.

The connection between Bert and AIDS spun off into another bizarre story that Bert and Ernie, who lived together for years, were gay and soon to be married on TV. This urban legend began as a satire that people took to be the truth. In 1980 a humor writer named Kurt Anderson wrote a glib article with the following joking comments: "Bert and Ernie conduct themselves in the same loving, discreet way that millions of gay men, women, and hand puppets do. They do their jobs well and live a splendidly settled life together in an impeccably decorated cabinet." [46]

Inexplicably, this story was taken as a statement of fact by some homophobic readers. By 1993 the urban legend was so widespread that *TV Guide* began receiving letters protesting the homosexual relationship of Bert and Ernie. A year later, a radio preacher in North Carolina started a campaign urging his listeners to write letters to the producers of *Sesame Street* demanding the removal of Bert and Ernie because of their alleged homosexuality. This fueled rumors that the touring company of *Sesame Street* was going to put on a skit in which the male Muppets were married. Forced to respond to these urban legends, the Children's Television Workshop sent out a press release that stated, "Bert and Ernie, who've been on *Sesame Street* for 25 years, do not portray a gay couple and there are no plans for them to do so in the future. They are puppets, not humans."[47]

Bert and Ernie (far left), Sesame Street pals for twenty-five years, became the targets of urban legends after creator Jim Henson died in 1990.

Dizzy Disney Myths

In the strange world of urban legends, even two-dimensional characters can become the source of controversy and myth. This happened to the cartoon character Aladdin, who appeared in the Walt Disney Company animated film of the same name. Similar to the *Sesame Street* story, the *Aladdin* urban legend was fueled by people looking for suggestive messages behind the most innocent of characters.

The *Aladdin* controversy began in the early 1990s when the cartoon was released on video. This allowed viewers to slow down and repeat a specific scene that was found to be controversial by some. In the scene, Aladdin tries to impress a female character named Jasmine by flying up to the girl's balcony on a magic carpet. However, when the young man steps onto the balcony, Jasmine's tiger, Rajah, growls and threatens to attack. What happens next has been the source of a persistent legend circulated by some unlikely organizations. As Aladdin tries to chase off the tiger with his turban, he utters a single line. Urban legend has it that Aladdin says, "All good teenagers, take off your clothes."[48] The Walt Disney Company strongly denies the rumor, saying that Aladdin actually said "Scat, good tiger, take off and go!"[49]

The denial did little to squelch the urban legend, which became so prevalent that it was covered by the *Wall Street Journal*. As reporter Lisa Bannon writes:

> In the case of "Aladdin," the allegation crisscrossed the country, traveling mostly through conservative Christian circles and helped by, among others, Mrs. [Anna] Runge; a high-school biology class in Owensboro, [Kentucky]; an Iowa college student; and a traveling troupe of evangelical actors. It was passed on by some people who didn't believe it, by others who thought it was a joke, and by a Christian magazine that later—and apparently to no effect—retracted its

Weird Walt Disney Legends

Walt Disney, founder of the Walt Disney Company, was a creative pioneer. Over the years, he was responsible for inventing the characters Mickey Mouse and Donald Duck. Disney also created dozens of critically acclaimed, long-running TV shows, dozens of full-length animated films such as *Fantasia* and *The Lion King*, and the world's first theme park, Disneyland. Like other figures beloved by the public, Disney was also the subject of some bizarre legends that persisted long after his death.

The fact that Disneyland is full of futuristic, robotic creatures gave rise to the rumor that Disney had his body cryogenically frozen when he died of cancer in 1966. It is said that his relatives will bring him back to life when medical technology has found a cure for cancer. The source for this widely held, but false, belief remains a mystery.

Another associated legend holds that Disney made a film to be shown after his death to instruct executives on how to run the Walt Disney Company well into the future. The theme of running the company from beyond the grave is also seen in the Disney Will rumor. This alleged will is said to include a list of Disney films that should never be released on video, even though home videos did not exist at the time of his death.

In reality, the Walt Disney Company was a publicly held corporation and Walt did not hold a controlling share, nor was he even on the board of directors. The urban legends concerning him are as fantastical as a Disney cartoon.

story. At least two waves of the rumor swept the country, from very different starting points. [50]

While many urban legends have mysterious beginnings, it appears that those spreading the Disney hoax had a political agenda. The legend was perpetuated by a religious group called American Life League, based in Stafford, Virginia, that was promoting a boycott of Disney because the company distributed films the group found offensive.

After the American Life League printed a newsletter with the myth about the cartoon, the story was picked up by a magazine published in Atlanta called *Movie Guide*, which bills itself as a Christian entertainment publication. The story titled "Aladdin Exposed" says that the message in *Aladdin* is similar to the alleged subliminal messages hidden in heavy metal rock songs, which could only be heard by playing the songs backward or at a different speed. The article says that Disney included the message for nefarious purposes and urged its readers to write letters of protest to then–Disney chairman Michael Eisner. The message spread across America, and Disney offices were flooded with letters. However, the *Movie Guide* quickly retracted its story after being presented with digital copies of the soundtrack in which the alleged offending words were obviously not uttered. Although Disney cleared the air of the allegations, the urban legend continues today.

Rock and Roll Rumors

Urban legends about cartoon characters and other childhood icons are difficult for some to believe. Most people simply do not accept the indecencies assigned to innocent characters. Legends about rock and roll performers, however, are much easier for many to accept. Over the years, rock stars have been known to drink too much, take massive amounts of drugs, and get caught performing all manner of sexual indiscretions. Musicians have smashed their equipment, decapitated bats with their teeth, and shouted obscenities onstage. And their offstage antics have been even more shocking. This is conceivably why people will believe almost any outlandish urban legend about a rock and roll musician.

When a band's stage act is built around shocking audiences, it is even harder for people to separate fact from fiction. Until the 1970s, the most outrageous things seen onstage were Jimi Hendrix setting his guitar on fire, members of the Who destroying their amplifiers and drums, or Janis Joplin drinking an entire bottle of Southern Comfort liquor. So when Alice Cooper came along in the early seventies, people were taken aback when he dressed as a transgender vampire and spilled gallons of fake blood, handled live snakes, and pretended to have his head chopped off in a fake guillotine.

Although Cooper's performance was an act, the urban legends began almost immediately. It was said that the rocker threw a bag full of kittens into a crowd and instructed people to tear them apart, or he would not go on with the show. Another rumor started when a fan actually threw a live chicken onstage. Cooper, thinking it would fly away, threw it back into the crowd, where it was immediately torn

Shock rocker Alice Cooper's outrageous persona made it easy for legend creators to spin crazy tales about him.

apart. The next day, the press reported that Cooper bit the chicken's head off and drank its blood. The story has persisted for years. Cooper's advisor, however, realized that there was money to be made from such legends. When controversial rock musician Frank Zappa heard the chicken story, he asked Cooper if it was true. When Cooper said no, Zappa replied, "Well, whatever you do, don't tell anybody you didn't do it."[51]

I Buried Paul

That outlandish rock acts breed peculiar legends may not be surprising. However, the source of one of the biggest rock and roll urban legends of all time, that Beatles bass player Paul McCartney is dead, remains a mystery. And the dozens of clues assembled by Beatles fans allegedly proving McCartney's death seemed undeniably true to many. As Toropov writes,

> In the annals of popular music, no urban legend has been more enduring, more intricately debated, and . . . more fascinating than this one. The tale of Paul McCartney's supposed death and replacement by a clone . . . refuses to go away. For most observers, though, the pertinent question is . . . "Where on earth did this story come from?"[52]

During the 1960s, the Beatles were the most successful rock band in the world. When they first appeared in the United States in early 1964, they were instantly adored for their innocent charm, shaggy haircuts, and polished and intelligent songs. By the end of the decade, however, the Beatles, like millions of their fans, had become hippies. They took drugs, grew long hair and beards, and let it be known that they opposed the Vietnam War. In the space of six years, the group had gone from innocent songsters to symbols of the counterculture rebellion.

Sometime around September 1969, Beatles fans began hearing that the band's bass player, Paul McCartney, had died in a grisly auto accident and was replaced by a clone. At the time, Beatles albums were often closely examined by fans. Every picture, word, and sound effect was analyzed for hidden meanings. When the Paul Is Dead story broke, fans were in a frenzy coming up with clues. The clues were passed around like the latest Beatles albums until the urban legend became a media sensation. At its height, thousands of people were calling Apple, the Beatles' record company, every day while the story was reported in over three hundred newspapers and covered by all the major television networks.

The earliest clues of Paul being dead appear on the 1967 album *Sgt. Pepper's Lonely Hearts Club Band*. On the inside jacket of the album, McCartney is wearing a band uniform with the letters O.P.D., which purportedly mean "Officially Pronounced Dead." (The acronym really stands for Ontario Police Department.)

The cover photo of the album *Abbey Road* is said to be rife with clues that proved McCartney was dead. In the picture, the band is walking across London's Abbey Road, in front of the Abbey Road Studio, where the album was recorded. The photo shows McCartney as the only barefoot member of the band. This is supposed to relate to an Italian practice of burying bodies with no shoes. The other members of the band are said to be dressed as part of a funeral party. George Harrison is wearing the jeans and work shirt of a grave digger; Ringo Starr is dressed in black as a mourner; and John Lennon is dressed in a suit as one who officiates at a funeral. A Volkswagen parked nearby has the license number 28 IF. This is said to mean that McCartney would have been twenty-eight years old if he lived.

Mysteriously recorded lyrics also play a part in this urban legend. The Beatles were famous for placing inside jokes, unusual sound effects, and backward lyrics in some of their

Shock Rock Rumors that Refuse to Die

Like many urban legends that refuse to die, those applied to shock rocker Alice Cooper in the 1970s remained alive until they could be applied to another extreme rock star, Marilyn Manson, in the 1990s. Like Cooper, Manson has been accused of torturing dogs or kittens and tossing them into the audience. In a 1998 interview, quoted in the Urban Legends Reference Pages on snopes.com, Cooper comments on the resilience of such urban legends:

> I hear 10 Marilyn Manson rumors a day. I used to hear that many Alice Cooper rumors. I never set a German shepherd on fire. We had the kitten thing, too. . . . Here's another one: Marilyn Manson's father was [children's television host] Captain Kangaroo. It was in every newspaper that my father was Mr. Green Jeans (Captain Kangaroo's sidekick). Every time I hear a new Marilyn Manson story, I can tell you what's going to happen next because I'll tell you what happened to me.

Marilyn Manson is now the subject of legends once attributed to Alice Cooper.

songs. The hit single "Strawberry Fields Forever," written by Lennon, demonstrates this. At the end of the swirling kaleidoscopic song as the sound effects fade out, Lennon's voice is heard at a slow speed, allegedly saying "I buried Paul."[53]

On "I'm So Tired," another song by Lennon on the 1969 *White Album*, the singer mumbles an incoherent phrase at the end of the song. When played backward, some believed

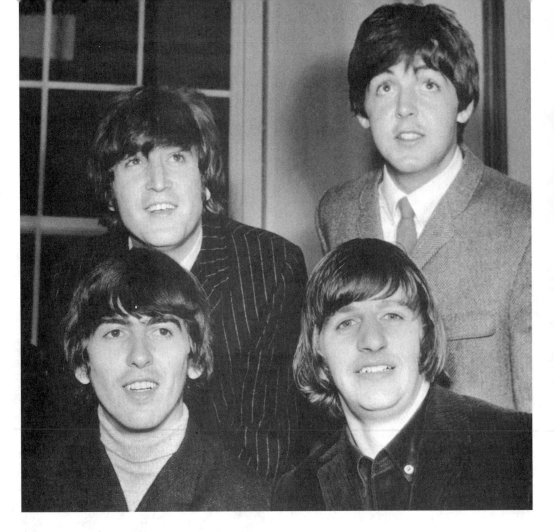

Fans found many supposed clues in Beatles' song lyrics to support the rumor that Beatle Paul McCartney (upper right) had died in the 1960s.

Lennon said, "Paul is dead, man, miss him, miss him."[54] On yet another Lennon song on the *White Album*, "Revolution 9," the singer chants, "number 9, number 9," over and over. Played backward, this purportedly sounds like "Turn me on, dead man."[55]

While the Paul Is Dead legend was repeated around the world, McCartney was mysteriously absent from the scene. Since he had been in the public eye nearly nonstop for years, fans wondered why he did not simply give an interview and stop the rumors. Eventually, the famous Beatle briefly emerged from seclusion at his manor in Scotland. Although he did not address the many alleged clues that proved his death, his appearance served to squelch the rumors.

The urban legends concerning McCartney's demise remain alive even today. At least a dozen Web sites have been published to cast light on the "clues." It is obvious to those who publish this material that the Beatle never really died. McCartney was performing concerts throughout the world in 2005, reminding urban legend fans of the line spoken by author Mark Twain in 1897: "Rumors of my death have been greatly exaggerated."[56] While Twain's statement is not an urban legend, great exaggerations, twisted truths, and outright lies are all part of a celebrity's life. Whether they play innocent kids on TV or fake their own deaths onstage, imaginations will run wild, people will talk, and urban legends about stars will continue on even after their careers are over.

Chapter 5

Criminal Acts and Gruesome Legends

Senseless, violent crimes have long been rampant in human societies. Throughout history, countless people have been beaten, raped, disfigured, and murdered by total strangers without explanation. In such a world, it is little wonder that the fear of violent crime holds a tight grip on the human psyche. The reality, however, is that random crime, while broadly feared, affects only a tiny percentage of the population. For example, in the United States, with a population of nearly 300 million people, less than fifteen thousand intentional homicides occur in an average year, and most of the victims knew their killers. As these statistics show, most people will go through life without ever having to face down knife-wielding slashers, ax murderers, or criminals brandishing large-caliber handguns. While people do see stories about brutal crimes in the media every day, the fact remains that these are isolated incidents that few need to fear.

Perhaps more puzzling than the fear of violent crime is the thrill people find in telling tales of horror, a kind of elation that is found when some ghastly act has happened to someone else. While there may be no explanation for this pleasure, there is no shortage of ghost stories, horror films, and urban legends concerned with random criminal acts and gruesome tortures of all kinds. Some tales serve as a warning, while others are just frightening or gross for the sake of sensationalism.

Maniacs on the Loose

Most criminal urban legends are similar to scary stories often told around campfires or at slumber parties. The tales most often involve teenagers alone on a dark night and fugitive killers or maniacs who have recently escaped from a

Fears of falling victim to a horrific crime lead many to accept as truth the outrageous claims of countless urban crime legends.

local mental institution. Like most other urban legends, they are often told along with the information that they really happened to a friend of a friend. However, as Brunvand writes in *Be Afraid, Be Very Afraid*, "While these stories are not literally true, any more than a horror film is, when hearing them we realize that they *could* be true."[57]

The classic urban legend of horror involves a beautiful teenage girl named Sara, who lives in a small town. Her parents go away and leave her home alone overnight. Although it is the first time Sara has been left alone, she has a large German shepherd to protect her. After her parents leave,

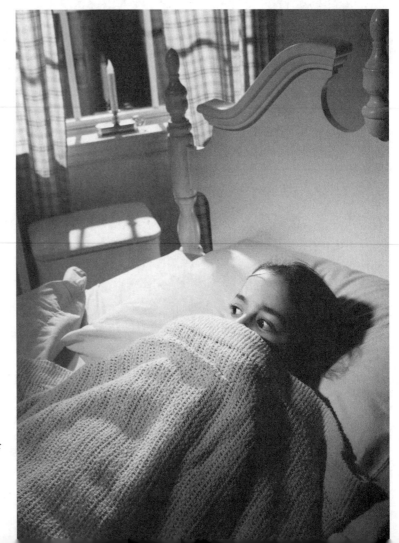

Many urban legends involve a beautiful teenage girl who is home alone and finds herself at the mercy of a psychotic killer.

Sara hears a news report that a maniac has escaped from the local insane asylum outside of town. He is on the loose and extremely dangerous. The report warns people to stay in their houses, and Sara makes sure all the doors and windows are locked tight. Although she is nervous, Sara goes to sleep and her dog accompanies her, going to sleep, as usual, under her bed. She awakens at 2 A.M. feeling scared. For reassurance, she puts her hand down and the dog licks it. She hears a weird dripping but decides to ignore it and go back to sleep. Several hours later, Sara, having a bad dream, wakes up again. Once again, she reaches over the edge of the bed and is reassured by the dog licking her hand.

By now, the dripping is really bothering Sara, so after checking to make sure all the faucets are turned off, she decides to sleep in the living room, where she cannot hear the annoying noise. Nevertheless, Sara wakes up early, at dawn, after a restless night. She returns to her room and calls to her dog. When he fails to crawl out from under the bed, Sara peeks beneath the mattress. She sees the dog dead with its jaw ripped off (so it could not bark) and blood dripping from its mangled face. Next to her bed, she spies a small note from the killer, written in blood, saying: "HUMANS CAN LICK TOO, MY BEAUTIFUL."[58]

The Licked Hand story, along with various alternate versions, is a classic urban legend for several reasons. It contains elements common to many legends—a psycho killer, a teenager home alone, and a grisly twist at the end. The story also contains elements of truth. Escaped killers do occasionally break into homes. That these isolated events are often given wide coverage in the media helps add to the believability factor of the Licked Hand. In addition, the story serves as a parable—the maniac must have sneaked into Sara's house before she secured the doors and windows. Her hairbreadth escape can serve as a warning to others to lock up when home alone.

A Gang Initiation from Ancient Rome

The Lights Out gang initiation legend first circulated in the early 1990s. However, stories about gang initiations can be traced back at least to ancient Rome. In 63 B.C. the author Minucius described a gang ritual involving a baby's murder in the book *Octavius*. While the legend was believed to be widely accepted as truth, it was debunked soon after it circulated. The legend is reprinted in *Aliens, Ghosts, and Cults*, by Bill Ellis:

Details of the initiation of [new gang members] are as revolting as they are notorious.

An infant, cased in [bread] dough to deceive the unsuspecting, is placed beside the person to be initiated. The novice is thereupon induced to inflict what seem to be harmless blows upon the dough, and unintentionally the infant is killed by his unsuspecting blows; the blood—oh, horrible—they lap up greedily; the limbs they tear to pieces eagerly; and over the victim they make league and covenant, and by complicity in guilt pledge themselves to mutual silence. Such sacred rites are more foul than any sacrilege.

The Lights Out Legend

While some people might believe Sara's story, it has more resemblance to a horror movie than to real life. Other types of urban legends, however, are more grounded in reality. Yet they seem to exist only to exploit people's fears for no apparent reason. A classic example surfaced in late 1993 when the deeds of criminal street gangs were receiving a great deal of attention in the media. At this time, the Internet was in its infancy, and the only people with e-mail were a limited number of academics and businesspeople. However, a legend quickly spread via e-mail in the United States and Canada that, as part of an initiation, gang members were intentionally driving at night with their lights off. The story claims that when a helpful citizen in an oncoming car flashed his or her lights to alert the driver, the gang member took this as an invitation to turn the "lights out,"[59] or kill the victim. The warnings, which were printed on flyers and circulated by fax and e-mail, cautioned readers not to flash their car lights at anyone.

The Lights Out story took on new life when someone faxed a letter to the Chicago Police Department warning that the weekend of September 25–26 was going to be Lights Out Weekend. The letter purported that during that time, the Black Gangster Disciple Nation gang was going to commit random murders across the United States when people flashed their car lights at them. A similar message appeared on flyers placed in the mailboxes of employees at the University of California in Irvine, near Los Angeles. However, the California initiation was alleged to be carried out by the Bloods gang.

While police had to take such warnings seriously, a search of newspaper stories and police records found no mention of this random terrorist act actually taking place. However, stories began to circulate that several Lights Out murders had already been committed. At Queens College in New York City, bulletin boards across the campus were covered with photocopied warnings about a series of Lights Out murders, said to be based on information from the

One urban legend from the 1990s warned drivers that if they flashed their headlights at cars driving with their lights out, gang members would kill them.

Queens Borough commander of the New York Police Department. Similar posters were put up in New Jersey and elsewhere. It remains a mystery as to how or why the legend spread, as college professor and urban legend researcher Pamela Donovan writes in *No Way of Knowing:*

> The common denominator in all of the disseminated warnings—those spread by word-of-mouth, those publicized through duplicated leaflets, and those transmitted electronically—is that no evidence exists to date that any of them described real threats or events, nor were they presented as such in public forums such as law enforcement warnings or news media accounts. Fictional police officers, security personnel, and news media references do often appear, however, in these photocopied and e-mail texts.[60]

Not only did the media not spread the legend, but many members of the press tried to debunk it. *New York Newsday* published an article labeling the Lights Out story a hoax, as did the San Jose *Mercury News*, the *Atlantic City Press*, and the *Milwaukee Journal*. Despite these news stories, authorities continued to receive frantic calls about the threat. Police told callers that the story was false; however, as Donovan writes, the media and police were not needed to perpetuate the rumor. It was "reliant upon anonymous tips, authorless texts, word-of-mouth, and ill-defined whisper campaigns about unspecific perpetrators and victims."[61]

Abduction Legends

While the Lights Out story focuses on the general public's fears of black street gangs, racial themes pervade another widespread urban legend, sometimes called the abduction legend. This story was popularized in the late 1960s in France, when it was said that innocent young girls were being drugged while shopping in dress boutiques owned by Jewish merchants. The girls were then shipped abroad and forced to work as prostitutes. At the height of the rumor, the anti-Semitic overtones of the legend prompted several acts of violence against Jewish shop owners in Orleans, France.

The abduction legend was hardly new at the time of the attacks. In fact, it can be traced back to Great Britain in the 1880s, when there was extensive fear that proper Victorian ladies were at risk of being abducted by Chinese opium addicts and sold into what was then called the "white slave" market.

The abduction legend was updated to modern America in the 1970s, when the place of the kidnappings moved from dress shops to shopping mall restrooms. The women in this story were most often beautiful blond teenage girls who

A Twist on the Abduction Legend

The rumor that young women were being kidnapped and forced into prostitution dates back to the 1880s. Like many urban legends that refuse to die, this story gets updated every few years. In recent times, an e-mail version of the abduction legend combined fear of men from the Middle East with family fun at Disneyland. The legend is reprinted in *No Way of Knowing*, by Pamela Donovan:

Has anyone heard about the kidnapping that almost took place at DL [Disneyland]? Apparently a woman and her child (either age 4, 5, or 6) were sitting on the curb on main street, the mother turned her head just for a second and looked back for her child and he was gone. She then frantically [alerted] security. They took her to an office where there were quite a few t.v. monitors to look for her

son. She was so out of breath and [distraught] security told her that they didn't have much time, that to look closely at faces not at the clothes her child was wearing or his hair. From the time she entered the office, they found her child in a matter of 3 minutes. He was headed out the entrance by a couple of Iranians. When they grabbed him they took him to a restroom and changed his clothes and shaved his head, all in a matter of minutes. That way he wouldn't be noticed. [Their] reason for taking him was so that they could sell him.

This just sends chills up my spine. I have 3 children 7, 4, 2. The moral of this sad story is that when ever you are in the park keep your child at your side at all times, to prevent this ever happening to you.

were drugged with either heroin, cocaine, or LSD in public bathrooms. Another version claimed that the drug was injected into the victim's buttocks through the crack in a folding theater seat. Sometimes information was added that the predators were either gangsters, members of a religious cult, a group of hippies, or men disguised as women.

In November 1980, the abduction legend caused widespread panic in Madison, Wisconsin. However, it remained a mystery to authorities as to how, why, or where the urban legend became so firmly established. According to an article in the Madison *Capital Times,*

> Madison police and shopping center officials are becoming increasingly disturbed over a plague of rumors circulating that young girls are being drugged and abducted from shopping centers.

> The rumors began circulating about five weeks ago when a [false] story made the rounds that a teen-age girl was shot full of heroin in a restroom at West Towne [shopping center], and was being carried away by two women when she was rescued by relatives and taken to a hospital for treatment. [62]

In the early 1990s, when several high-profile child abduction stories were in the news, the victims in the abduction legend morphed from teenage girls to young children. In these stories, the mothers either looked away "for just a second" [63] or were trying on clothes when their three- or four-year-old children vanished. Security guards were notified, and a frantic search was conducted.

In a story meant to dispel belief in urban legends, *McCall's* magazine quoted other erroneous elements of the story:

> [Authorities] were about to give up when one of the guards found the girl standing on a toilet in the men's restroom so you couldn't see her feet. Her long, dark

hair had been chopped off and dyed blond, and she was dressed in boys clothes! Apparently she had been abducted by a notorious child-snatching ring who abandoned her once they realized the search was on. [64]

Such "child snatching" groups are said to sell children as slaves, sexually exploit them, or run black-market adoption rings.

The various abduction myths became a staple of Internet newsgroups in the second half of the 1990s. As the popularity of digital communication expanded, so did the numbers of postings concerning the abduction legends, especially in online parents groups. Donovan's research into the matter found over 220 references to the urban legend in various newsgroups in 1996, 360 the next year, 591 in 1997, and 690 in 1998. Although debunked time and again by media sources and authorities, the legend continued to concern thousands of parents who never questioned the logic of a child disappearing when parents look away "for just a few seconds."

Black Market Kidneys

While stories of losing innocent children are fearsome, macabre legends of people losing body parts are simply grotesque. Yet a nightmarish legend about a man whose kidney is stolen was widely circulated—and apparently taken as fact—beginning in the early 1990s. The story begins in New Orleans, Louisiana, during the annual Mardi Gras celebration. A man named William Rowe is in town for business but soon joins the huge street party. After drinking too much, Rowe is approached by a woman who seduces him. However, Rowe quickly passes out, only to awake the next morning in his hotel room. He looks around and notices he is sitting in the bathtub, which is filled with ice cubes. While trying to pull his freezing body out of the tub, the businessman notices that a chair and the telephone from the other room have been pulled into the bathroom. A note is

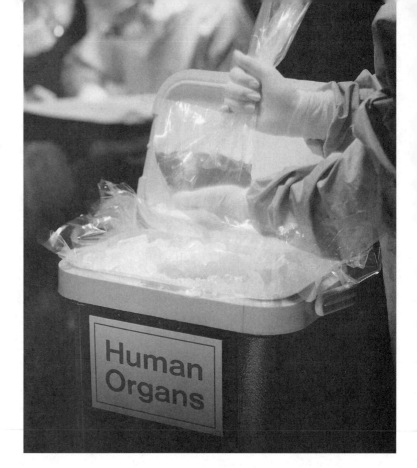

The need for organs for transplants, such as the heart shown in this photo, inspired a legend about black-market kidney thieves.

taped to the chair that reads, "Dear Sir, Reach behind you and feel your back. You need to see a doctor immediately. Do not move. Do not leave the tub. . . . Call 911. You have been warned!"[65]

Rowe feels his back and finds a tube protruding from a surgical incision. After dialing 911, he is again warned, by the emergency operator, not to leave the tub; the operator assures him an ambulance is on the way. When emergency personnel arrive, instead of exhibiting shock, they seem unfazed by the man's bizarre situation. At the hospital, doctors also act as if nothing is remarkable about Rowe's involuntary hotel room surgery. Finally, Rowe learns that the woman drugged him, an unscrupulous doctor removed one (or both, in some versions) of his kidneys, and his pilfered organ is probably now for sale on the medical black market for $10,000.

Alternate versions of the Stolen Kidney story are circulated in which the victim wakes up in blood-soaked sheets in Las Vegas or New York City. The warning note is sometimes written in lipstick on the mirror. One written warning that circulated with the Stolen Kidney story contained additional information:

> [This is] to warn you about a new crime ring that is targeting business travelers. This ring is well organized, well-funded, has very skilled personnel, and is currently operating in most major cities and recently very active in New Orleans. . . . This is not a scam or out of a science fiction novel, it is real. It is documented and confirmable. If you travel or someone close to you travels, please be careful.[66]

Nothing explains why someone would circulate a flyer claiming the story to be "documented and confirmable." However, e-mail versions of the story also contained misinformation intended to verify it. Reproduced in the Urban Legends Reference Pages, a letter allegedly from someone named Patty Radford states, "Yes, this does happen. My sister-in-law works with a lady [and] this happened to her son's neighbor who lives in Houston." Another from Kathy White says, "My husband is a Houston Firefighter/EMT and they have received alerts regarding this crime ring. . . . The daughter of a friend of a fellow firefighter had this happen to her."[67]

Such information about a horrible event actually happening to a friend of a friend—or a relative of a friend of a friend—is a staple of urban legends. This source was even mentioned when the Stolen Kidney story made it on to prime-time television. The legend was the plot of an episode of the crime drama *Law and Order* called "Sonata for Solo Organ." When the writer of the story was asked how he came up with the idea, he said he heard that it actually happened to a friend of a friend.

Whatever the source, the Stolen Kidney story, while never documented as true, acts as a modern-day parable. It warns against being unwary in unfamiliar cities, drinking too much, and trusting strangers, especially women who seem overly friendly for no clear reason. The legend is also a commentary on the selfishness of society at large—there is such a shortage of organ donors that black marketers can make large sums of money trafficking in stolen body parts.

Harvesting Organs of Children

While the Stolen Kidney story is most often circulated in industrial nations by fax, flyer, and e-mail, the story is also popular in developing nations, where it is dispersed by word of mouth. The victims in these rumors are often homeless children who are either mutilated or killed so that thieves can steal their eyes, livers, kidneys, or hearts.

While it might be a mystery that someone would believe such a story in North America or Europe, some people in poverty-stricken nations consider organ theft to be just one more among the countless horrors they face every day. As medical researcher Nancy Scheper-Hughes writes in *Natural History* magazine, "[Urban legends] about organ stealing can be heard among poor people in Brazil. The rumors are based on similar perceptions—equally grounded in . . . reality—that their lives and those of their children are dispensable."[68] This attitude may be seen among the poor in Guatemala, where many believe the urban legend that white American tourists are adopting Guatemalan children in order to harvest their organs. This story is nothing new, however. In the sixteenth century, indigenous Mayans in Guatemala believed that the lighter-skinned Spanish conquistadors were anemic. It was said that the invaders drained the blood of Mayan babies, hoping to cure the disease.

In more recent times, when a substantial number of Guatemalans embraced communism, the stolen body parts

"An Urban Myth Run Amok"

By 1997 so many people believed the story about thieves stealing kidneys from unsuspecting travelers that the National Kidney Foundation, which promotes kidney health and (voluntary) organ donation, was forced to issue the following statement on its Web site, www.kidney.org:

A persistent rumor that has been circulating for the past ten years has recently been reborn on the Internet: a business traveler has a drink with a stranger and wakes up in a tub full of ice, minus both kidneys.

The foundation has received calls from concerned business travelers who have been warned by their travel agents to beware of this 'crime ring' when traveling. "It's an urban myth run amok," says Dr. Wendy Brown, chairman of the National Kidney Foundation. "There is no evidence that such activity has ever occurred in the United States." . . .

"It is unfortunate when inaccurate information is reported about the Organ and Tissue Donor process," states Dr. Brown. "In truth, transplanting a kidney from a living donor involves numerous tests for compatibility that must be performed before the kidney is removed. So it's highly unlikely that a gang could operate in secrecy to recover organs that would be viable for a transplant." . . .

In an effort to dispel this urban myth, the National Kidney Foundation is asking any individual who claims to have had his or her kidneys illegally removed to step forward and contact the foundation.

Dr. Brown is concerned that the unfortunate hoax will affect the public's willingness to become Organ and Tissue Donors at a time when more than 50,000 Americans are awaiting life-saving organ transplants and nine to 10 people on the waiting list die each day.

legend was used to make the political point that capitalism was so corrupt that people would even steal kidneys to make a profit. As Véronique Campion-Vincent writes in *Western Folklore* magazine, the story "was initially accepted in many intellectual circles, not because of propaganda machines, but because of its own exemplary value. It was a horror that was plausible to . . . committed enemies of capitalism because this plundering and dismemberment of innocent humans seemed to parallel the plundering of raw materials by developed countries."[69]

In other nations, the fear of organ theft among the poor can cause significant changes in behavior, some of them fatal. As Scheper-Hughes writes, "Because of these rumors, shantytown residents in Brazil try to avoid public hospitals, where they fear they will die prematurely so that their organs may be harvested."[70]

While skeptics may scoff at this belief, it is grounded in reality. As early as 1800, students in Great Britain created a demand for fresh corpses, which were needed for medical experimentation. A gang of dealers in body parts was eventually convicted of murdering at least seventy homeless people in order to sell the cadavers to medical schools. In recent years, the severe shortage of organs for transplants has created a market for various body parts. In India, China, and other impoverished nations, people voluntarily line up at

Chinese police officers practice executing prisoners with a shot to the head. Chinese police are instructed to shoot the head to keep organs intact for harvesting.

hospitals, willing to part with a kidney or an eyeball for less than $1,000. These are later sold to rich people for up to $100,000. In China, another chilling chapter in the true story of harvested organs comes from jails where condemned prisoners are executed by gunshots to the head so that their organs will be undamaged. As Donovan writes, "Most other methods of execution ruin the organs, and since the Chinese government profits from selling organs of executed prisoners to wealthy people in need who check into Beijing hospitals, most are executed by gun."[71]

As actual practices in China demonstrate, there is a fine line between the horrors of the real world and the ghastly tales chronicled in urban legends. Perhaps that is why so many accept the scary, creepy, and disgusting behavior illustrated by legends. They serve as a way to cope with the harsh realities of life. As Dégh writes, "Speaking the language of concern, fear, and pain, legends reveal the desperate attempts that people make . . . to survive on the planet Earth . . . by rationalizing the irrational."[72] In this way, urban legends can turn horrid behavior into sick jokes that allow people to deal with death, or as macabre filmmaker Tim Burton says, "whistle past the graveyard."[73] If so, urban legends may serve to help some people conquer their deepest fears with nothing more than a nervous laugh. And as long as people continue to harbor deep dread of the unknown, urban legends will likely be told well into the foreseeable future.

Notes

Introduction: Stories, Rumors, and Urban Legends

1. Barbara Mikkelson and David P. Mikkelson, "Urban Legends Reference Pages: Critter Country," snopes.com, 2003. www.snopes.com/critters.
2. Linda Dégh, *Legend and Belief*. Bloomington, IN: Indiana University Press, 2001, p. 2.
3. Quoted in Jan Harold Brunvand, *Too Good to Be True: The Colossal Book of Urban Legends*. New York: W.W. Norton, 1999, p. 19.
4. Jan Harold Brunvand, *The Vanishing Hitchhiker*. New York: W.W. Norton, 1981, p. xiii.
5. Quoted in Jan Harold Brunvand, *The Encyclopedia of Urban Legends*. Santa Barbara: ABC-CLIO, 2001, p. xxviii.

Chapter One: Animal Myths

6. Mikkelson and Mikkelson, "Urban Legends Reference Pages: Critter Country."
7. Marie-Louise von Franz, *Shadow and Evil in Fairy Tales*. London: Shambhala, 1995, pp. 145–46.
8. Native American Lore Index, "The Buffalo and the Field Mouse," 1996. www.ilhawaii.net/~stony/lore01.html.

9. Jan Harold Brunvand, *The Mexican Pet*. New York: W.W. Norton, 1986, p. 41.
10. Quoted in Brunvand, *The Mexican Pet*, p. 8.
11. Quoted in Brunvand, *The Mexican Pet*, p. 8.
12. Quoted in Paul Smith, ed., *Perspectives on Contemporary Legend*. Sheffield, England: University of Sheffield, 1984, p. 81.
13. Quoted in Brunvand, *The Mexican Pet*, p. 10.
14. Mikkelson and Mikkelson, "Urban Legends Reference Pages."
15. Quoted in Jan Harold Brunvand, *Be Afraid, Be Very Afraid*. New York: W.W. Norton, 2004, p. 117.
16. Quoted in Brunvand, *Too Good to Be True*, p. 185.

Chapter Two: Food Fears and Fantasies

17. Quoted in CNN.com, "Officials: Diner Finds Finger in Chili," March 24, 2005. www.cnn.com/2005/US/03/24/chili.finger.reut.
18. Matthew, "Urban Legend Accidentally Comes True," SlashNot, March 2005. www.slashnot.com/article.php3?story_id=513.

19. Bill Ellis, *Aliens, Ghosts, and Cults*. Jackson: University Press of Mississippi, 2001, p. 162.

20. Quoted in Smith, ed., *Perspectives on Contemporary Legend*, pp. 135–36.

21. Quoted in Jan Harold Brunvand, *The Choking Doberman and Other "New" Urban Legends*. New York: W.W. Norton, 1984, p. 116.

22. Mikkelson and Mikkelson, "Urban Legends Reference Pages."

23. Quoted in Brandon Toropov, *The Complete Idiot's Guide to Urban Legends*. Indianapolis: Alpha, 2001, p. 115.

24. Quoted in Toropov, *The Complete Idiot's Guide to Urban Legends*, p. 115.

25. Quoted in David Emery, "Coke Adds Death," About: Urban Legends and Folklore, 2005. http://urbanlegends.about.com/library/blcoke.htm.

26. Quoted in David Emery, "The Curse of Frankenchicken," About: Urban Legends and Folklore, January 5, 2000. http://urbanlegends.about.com/library/weekly/aa010500a.htm?once=true&.

27. University of New Hampshire, "Kentucky Fried Chicken Hoax," March 16, 2000. www.unh.edu/Boiler Plate/kfc.html.

28. University of New Hampshire, "Kentucky Fried Chicken Hoax."

29. Toropov, *The Complete Idiot's Guide to Urban Legends*, p. 117.

30. Mark Twain, "Twain on Lies," Cafe Press, 2005. www.cafepress.com/sisyphus/211519.

Chapter Three: Government Conspiracies

31. Gary Alan Fine and Patricia A. Turner, *Whispers on the Color Line*. Berkeley: University of California Press, 2001, p. 113.

32. Quoted in David Emery, "Roswell: Birth of a Legend," About: Urban Legends and Folklore, 2005. http://urbanlegends.about.com/library/weekly/aa070697.

33. Quoted in Emery, "Roswell: Birth of a Legend."

34. saveinhere.com, "The Grand Conspiracy." www.saveinhere.com/ufo/ufo57.html.

35. saveinhere.com, "The Grand Conspiracy."

36. Emery, "Roswell: Birth of a Legend."

37. Quoted in Patricia A. Turner, *I Heard It Through the Grapevine*. Berkeley: University of California Press, 1993, pp. 74–75.

38. U.S. Senate Select Committee on Intelligence, "Intelligence Activities and the Rights of Americans," Paul Wolf's Web site, April 26, 1976. www.icdc.com/~paul wolf/cointelpro/churchfinalreportIIa.htm.

39. Quoted in Turner, *I Heard It Through the Grapevine*, p. 154.

40. Turner, *I Heard It Through the Grapevine*, pp. 154–55.

41. Quoted in Fine and Turner, *Whispers on the Color Line*, p. 159.

42. Fine and Turner, *Whispers on the Color Line*, p. 164.

43. Quoted in Fine and Turner, *Whispers on the Color Line*, p. 164.

Chapter Four: Legends of Stage and Screen

44. Richard Roeper, *Hollywood Urban Legends*. Franklin Lakes, NJ: New Page, 2001, p. 9.
45. Mikkelson and Mikkelson, "Urban Legends Reference Pages."
46. Quoted in Roeper, *Hollywood Urban Legends*, p. 52.
47. Quoted in Roeper, *Hollywood Urban Legends*, p. 53.
48. Quoted in Lisa Bannon, "How a Rumor Spread About Subliminal Sex in Disney's 'Aladdin,'" *Wall Street Journal*, October 24, 1995. www.snopes.com/disney/info/aladwsj.htm.
49. Quoted in Bannon, "How a Rumor Spread About Subliminal Sex in Disney's 'Aladdin.'"
50. Bannon, "How a Rumor Spread About Subliminal Sex in Disney's 'Aladdin.'"
51. Quoted in Mikkelson and Mikkelson, "Urban Legends Reference Pages."
52. Toropov, *The Complete Idiot's Guide to Urban Legends*, p. 31.
53. Quoted in Toropov, *The Complete Idiot's Guide to Urban Legends*, p. 35.
54. Quoted in Toropov, *The Complete Idiot's Guide to Urban Legends*, p. 35.
55. Quoted in Toropov, *The Complete Idiot's Guide to Urban Legends*, p. 35.
56. Quoted in Roeper, *Hollywood Urban Legends*, p. 227.

Chapter Five: Criminal Acts and Gruesome Legends

57. Brunvand, *Be Afraid, Be Very Afraid*, p. 13.
58. Quoted in Toropov, *The Complete Idiot's Guide to Urban Legends*, p. 264.
59. Quoted in Pamela Donovan, *No Way of Knowing*. New York: Routledge, 2004, p. 2.
60. Donovan, *No Way of Knowing*, p. 2.
61. Donovan, *No Way of Knowing*, p. 3.
62. Quoted in Brunvand, *The Choking Doberman and Other "New" Urban Legends*, p. 79.
63. Quoted in Donovan, *No Way of Knowing*, p. 87.
64. Quoted in Donovan, *No Way of Knowing*, p. 87.
65. Quoted in N.E. Genge, *Urban Legends*. New York: Three Rivers, 2000, p. 83.
66. Quoted in Brunvand, *Be Afraid, Be Very Afraid*, pp. 224–25.
67. Quoted in Mikkelson and Mikkelson, "Urban Legends Reference Pages."
68. Nancy Scheper-Hughes, "Truth and Rumor on the Organ Trail," *Natural History*, October 1998, p. 52.
69. Véronique Campion-Vincent, "The Baby-Parts Story: A New Latin American Legend," *Western Folklore*, January 1990, p. 23.
70. Scheper-Hughes, "Truth and Rumor on the Organ Trail."
71. Donovan, *No Way of Knowing*, p. 69.
72. Dégh, *Legend and Belief*, p. 442.
73. Quoted in Associated Press, "An Eccentric Man Addresses Hard Truths," CNN.com, January 13, 2004. www.cnn.com/2004/SHOWBIZ/Movies/01/13/film.tim.burton.ap.

For Further Reading

Books

Jan Harold Brunvand, *Be Afraid, Be Very Afraid*. New York: W.W. Norton, 2004. Written by the acknowledged expert in urban legends, this book contains updated versions of older legends along with newer tales that have been circulated by e-mail in recent years.

Thomas J. Craughwell, *Alligators in the Sewers and 222 Other Urban Legends*. New York: Black Dog & Leventhal, 1999. Stolen kidneys, murderers in the backseat, UFOs in New Mexico, and other classic urban legends are detailed in this book along with short explanations of their origins.

Alan Dundes and Carl R. Pagter, *Why Don't Sheep Shrink When It Rains?* Syracuse: University of Syracuse Press, 2000. A collection of humorous folklore that was circulated as fake memos, cartoons, faxes, and e-mail chain letters.

David Holt, *The Exploding Toilet: Modern Urban Legends*. Little Rock: August House, 2004. A collection of shocking, scary, and quirky urban legends, many of them with humorous or surprising twists at the end.

John Townsend, *Mysterious Urban Myths*. Chicago: Raintree, 2004. Shocking or scary legends concerning crimes, animals, medical mistakes, the supernatural, and other topics.

Web Sites

About: Urban Legends and Folklore (http://urbanlegends.about.com). A site with the latest urban legends, the top twenty-five legends, hoax photos, and other fascinating facts and fiction.

Native American Lore Index (www.ilhawaii.net/~stony/loreindx.html). A Web site with 150 traditional myths, legends, and parables from dozens of Indian tribes.

The Octopus's Garden, Paul Is Dead (www.rareexception.com/Garden/Beatles/Paul.php). A Web site with links to nine Beatles albums, each link containing alleged clues that Beatle Paul McCartney died in a car crash and was replaced by a clone.

Urban Legends Reference Pages (www.snopes.com). An up-to-date Web site with hundreds of urban legends, rated for truthfulness, in more than forty categories. Site also has a link to the twenty-five hottest legends, many circulated by e-mail.

Works Consulted

Books

Sabine Baring-Gould, *Curious Myths of the Middle Ages*. New Hyde Park, NY: University, 1967. Written in 1866, this book contains what might be called urban legends from centuries past. The author debunks what were once believed to be true stories about William Tell, the pied piper, the man in the moon, men with tails, and other stories with roots in the ancient past.

Jan Harold Brunvand, *Be Afraid, Be Very Afraid*. New York: W.W. Norton, 2004. A collection of scary urban legends featuring monsters, murderers, mutant insects, and other frightening beasts performing vile deeds.

————, *The Choking Doberman and Other "New" Urban Legends*. New York: W.W. Norton, 1984. This books gives details of urban legends, offers alternate versions, and attempts to trace the source of the stories by offering speculation from reporters and others with firsthand knowledge.

————, *The Encyclopedia of Urban Legends*. Santa Barbara: ABC-CLIO, 2001. This work is a major collection of legends from around the world arranged alphabetically in encyclopedic fashion.

————, *The Mexican Pet*. New York: W.W. Norton, 1986. Another group of bizarre stories from the urban legends authority, with chapters on animals, automobile stories, food contamination, sex, crime, and bad products.

————, *"Too Good to Be True: The Colossal Book of Urban Legends*. New York: W.W. Norton, 1999. Dozens of legends "as told to" famous people and the author concerning pets and insects, food fables, macabre horrors, contaminated food, and more.

————, *The Vanishing Hitchhiker*. New York: W.W. Norton, 1981. A study of American urban legends and their meaning with interpretations of the legends as folklore and cultural symbols.

Linda Dégh, *Legend and Belief*. Bloomington: Indiana University Press, 2001. A scholarly work that uncovers the roots of many urban myths in ancient legends and reveals the universal human concerns behind the stories.

Pamela Donovan, *No Way of Knowing*. New York: Routledge, 2004. A study of crime and the way it is portrayed in urban legends, especially those that circulate on the Internet.

Alan Dundes and Carl R. Pagter, *Urban Folklore from the Paperwork Empire*. Austin, TX: American Folklore Society, 1975. A collection of urban folklore concerning politics, racism, women's liberation, the military mentality, and sex that were circulated before the widespread use of the

Internet on handwritten letters, chain letters, memoranda, notices, and cartoons.

Bill Ellis, *Aliens, Ghosts, and Cults*. Jackson: University Press of Mississippi, 2001. A book that explores the links between urban legends and reality with examples of people performing bizarre acts, including cult rituals and murder after hearing about similar incidents in legends.

Gary Alan Fine and Patricia A. Turner, *Whispers on the Color Line*. Berkeley: University of California Press, 2001. An examination of urban legends and rumors told within black communities about government conspiracies, corporate wrongdoing, and gang violence.

Marie-Louise von Franz, *Shadow and Evil in Fairy Tales*. London: Shambhala, 1995. A study of common archetypal themes in fairy tales from around the world.

N.E. Genge, *Urban Legends*. New York: Three Rivers, 2000. A collection of more than three hundred modern myths from the humorous to the horrid that have made the rounds in offices, college dorms, and elsewhere.

Harrison Edward Livingstone, *Killing Kennedy and the Hoax of the Century*. New York: Carroll & Graf, 1995. Develops the theory that the famous "Zapruder film" showing Kennedy being shot is a fake that has been used to cover up what really happened.

Richard Roeper, *Hollywood Urban Legends*. Franklin Lakes, NJ: New Page, 2001. The stories and rumors that circulate about musicians, movie stars, television actors, and other rich and famous celebrities, written by the cohost of the TV show *Ebert & Roeper and the Movies*.

Paul Smith, ed., *Perspectives on Contemporary Legend*. Sheffield, England: University of Sheffield, 1984. Lectures about urban legends from prominent folklorists, delivered at the Conference for Contemporary Legends, sponsored by the Center for English Cultural Traditions and Language.

Brandon Toropov, *The Complete Idiot's Guide to Urban Legends*. Indianapolis: Alpha, 2001. A collection of legends concerning famous figures, paranoia, and scams, with information about the origin of the legend, how it was spread, and why it is false.

Patricia A. Turner, *I Heard It Through the Grapevine*. Berkeley: University of California Press, 1993. Urban legends particular to the African American community focusing on alleged conspiracies by racist hate groups, the U.S. government, and national corporations.

Johnny C. Young, *101 Popular Local Myths & Legends*. Manila: J.C. Young, 1996. A compilation of stories relating to the origins of people, places, animals, birds, and other things in the Philippines. It examines local customs, beliefs, and superstitions that have been retold for centuries.

Periodicals

Véronique Campion-Vincent, "The Baby-Parts Story: A New Latin American Legend," *Western Folklore*, January 1990.

Nancy Scheper-Hughes, "Truth and Rumor on the Organ Trail," *Natural History*, October 1998.

Internet Sources

Associated Press, "An Eccentric Man Addresses Hard Truths," CNN.com, January 13, 2004. www.cnn.com/2004/SHOWBIZ/Movies/01/13/film.tim.burton.ap.

Lisa Bannon, "How a Rumor Spread About Subliminal Sex in Disney's 'Aladdin,'" *Wall Street Journal*, October 24, 1995. www.snopes.com/disney/info/aladwsj.htm.

CNN.com, "Officials: Diner Finds Finger in Chili," March 24, 2005. www.cnn.com/2005/US/03/24/chili.finger.reut.

David Emery, "Coke Adds Death," About: Urban Legends and Folklore, 2005. http://urbanlegends.about.com/library/blcoke.htm.

———, "The Curse of Frankenchicken," About: Urban Legends and Folklore, January 5, 2000. http://urbanlegends. about. com/library/weekly/aa010500a.htm?once=true&.

———, "Roswell: Birth of a Legend," About: Urban Legends and Folklore, 2005. http://urbanlegends.about.com/library/weekly/aa070697.

Matthew (no last name given), "Urban Legend Accidentally Comes True," SlashNot, March 2005. www.slashnot.com/article.php3?story_id=513.

Barbara Mikkelson and David P. Mikkelson, "Urban Legends Reference Pages: Critter Country," snopes.com, 2003. www.snopes.com/critters.

National Kidney Foundation, "The National Kidney Foundation Dispels Rumors About Illegally Harvested Kidneys," April 4, 1997. www.kidney.org/general/news/newsitem.cfm?id=156.

Native American Lore Index, "The Buffalo and the Field Mouse," 1996. www.ilhawaii.net/~stony/lore01.html.

saveinhere.com, "The Grand Conspiracy," www.saveinhere.com/ufo/ufo57.html.

"Twain on Lies," Mark Twain, Cafe Press, 2005. www.cafepress.com/sisyphus/211519.

University of New Hampshire, "Kentucky Fried Chicken Hoax," March 16, 2000. www.unh.edu/BoilerPlate/kfc.html.

U.S. Senate Select Committee on Intelligence, "Intelligence Activities and the Rights of Americans," Paul Wolf's Website, April 26, 1976. www.icdc.com/~paulwolf/cointelpro/churchfinalreportIIa.htm.

Index

Picture Credits

Cover photo: © William Whitehurst/CORBIS
AP/Wide World Photos, 21, 29, 98
© Archivo Iconographico, S.A./CORBIS, 13
© Bettmann/CORBIS, 22, 49, 50, 82
Tim Boyle/Getty Images, 44
Joerg Carstensen/EPA/Landov, 81
Ben Edwards/Stone/Getty Images, 94
CBS/Landov, 69
Children's Television Workshop/Hulton Archive/Getty Images, 74
© CORBIS, 56
Tim Davis/Getty Images. 17
© Ferrell Grehan/CORBIS, 27
Dave Hogan/Hulton Archive/Getty Images, 78
Hulton Archive/Getty Images, 37
© Images.com/CORBIS, 52
John Kuntz/Reuters/Landov, 47
Erich Lessing/Art Resource, NY, 7
© Alexander Majewski/CORBIS, 85
Steve Marcus/Reuters/Landov, 31
Eric Miller/Getty Images, 34
Indranil Mukherjee/AFP/Getty Images, 43
Photos.com, 62, 89
© Robert Pickett/CORBIS, 10
Fred Prouser/Reuters/Landov, 72
Reuters/Landov, 55
Eufemio Rodriguez/DEX Images I/Dex Images/CORBIS, 86
Sion Touhig/Getty Images, 8
Brooke Slezak/Stone/Getty Images, 40
Francis Specker/Landov, 67
U.S. Census Bureau, 59

About the Author

Stuart A. Kallen is the author of more than two hundred nonfiction books for children and young adults. He has written on topics ranging from the theory of relativity to the history of rock and roll. In addition, Mr. Kallen has written award-winning children's videos and television scripts. In his spare time, he is a singer/songwriter/guitarist in San Diego, California.